TRYING TO BE GOOD

A BOOK ON *DOING* FOR THINKING PEOPLE

THOMAS E. SCHMIDT

Zondervan*PublishingHouse*
Academic and Professional Books
Grand Rapids, Michigan
A Division of HarperCollinsPublishers

TRYING TO BE GOOD
Copyright © 1990 by Thomas E. Schmidt

Requests for information should be addressed to:
Zondervan Publishing House
Academic and Professional Books
1415 Lake Drive S.E.
Grand Rapids, Michigan 49506

Library of Congress Cataloging-in-Publication Data

Schmidt, Thomas E.
Trying to be good : A book on *doing* for
thinking people / Thomas E. Schmidt.
p.   cm.
ISBN 0-310-52141-6
1. Christian ethics–Popular works.   2. Christian
ethics–Biblical teaching.
3. Ethics in the Bible.   I. Title.
BJ1261.S34   1990
241–dc20   90-35007
                                                        CIP

All Scripture quotations, unless otherwise noted, are from the
Holy Bible: New International Version (North American Edition).
Copyright © 1973, 1978, 1984 by the International Bible
Society. Used by permission of Zondervan Bible Publishers.

Edited by Gerard Terpstra and Leonard G. Goss

Printed in the United States of America

90 91 92 93 94 95 / CH / 10 9 8 7 6 5 4 3 2 1

• Contents •

• Foreword •

One of the most significant problems we Christians have to deal with is: "What does it mean to be spiritual?" I grew up, as did Dr. Schmidt, with a rather superficial answer to that question—"Keep these rules and you will be spiritual" my spiritual leaders said.

I soon found out that the problem of a spirituality defined by rule keeping was that it turned spirituality into a matter of doing the rules and failed to adequately address the ultimate question of being—who are you deep within yourself. Like the Pharisees of the New Testament, rule oriented spirituality misses the point. As Jesus suggested: you can keep all these rules and look very good on the outside but on the inside you are full of dead men's bones.

A second problem of rule-keeping spirituality is that it creates within us a false sense of our own goodness and thus prevents us from dealing with the deeper issues of true spirituality. This may be witnessed in people who keep the rules but lack charity and joy and overlook issues of justice and mercy.

Dr. Schmidt has done us a tremendous favor by wrestling with the problem of spirituality and ethics in a provocative and helpful way. He gets to the heart of the issue and presents us with a spiritual challenge that gets at our being—who we are in relation to God; and a spirituality that gets at an appropriate doing—who we are in our relation to other believers and to the world!

I believe this is a most timely book, especially for those who call themselves evangelical. In the past several decades American evangelical Christianity has been undergoing a significant shift, a shift that has divided evangelicals over the heart of the matter discussed by Dr. Schmidt. There are those who wish to return to the good old days when everyone kept the evangelical rule list, allowing easy distinction between those who were in and those who were out. But there are also many who wish to shift from the mere observance of rules to the development of the inner person.

This book speaks to this issue in a most constructive way and calls upon all Christians to pay attention to the issues that matter most—the calling to grow a character, a personality, and a style of life that takes its ultimate cue from the life and teachings of Jesus.

Robert E. Webber

• Preface •

A person from the midwest who moves to California reads about Paul's encounter with the Corinthians and senses that the New Testament world is not so foreign after all. My "Corinthians," the lively students of Westmont College, are working out their salvation in the midst of a culture where beliefs are privatized and immorality is publicized. They experience strong pressure to live with an ever-growing gap between right doctrine and right living. For Californians, then, and I suspect for others in "safer" places, a strong encouragement to turn beliefs into actions is potentially helpful. I have been driven by a conviction that this book needed to be written, and I am grateful to the Editor of Academic Books of Zondervan Publishing House for agreeing and for publishing a book that perhaps falls somewhere between scholarly and popular writing.

A number of individuals have contributed to the book, and they merit special thanks. J. I. Packer discussed the concept with me in the early stages and encouraged me concerning the need for such a book. Paul Ford and Dallas Willard provided helpful insights in advanced stages. Valerie Hahn offered detailed criticisms and insights that helped me to be more clear at many points. My wife, Catherine, was a faithful reader and critic even when the obligations of new motherhood required late-night reading. My daughter, Susanna, grew from a gleam in my eye to the apple of my eye in the time it took to complete this project, providing the encouragement of delight that only parents of toddlers can understand.

I dedicate the book to Mabel, a friend who died several years ago and whose life I describe in the last chapter. She is the only person I ever knew well who had no need to read this book, but she had a great part in the writing of it. I hope to thank her in person one of these days.

• Introduction •
How To Read This Book

It would be natural to begin a book about how people ought to live by asserting in the strongest possible terms my own ignorance, inexperience, and sinfulness. But those of my readers who know me need no convincing, and those who do not might only be convinced that I am terribly humble. In that case I would begin the book as a liar.

Perhaps the best way to introduce myself as an author of a book about behavior is to quote a cartoon character, Popeye the Sailor Man, who was famous for the phrase, "I yam what I yam." There is more than a difference in pronunciation between that simple claim and that of the Living God, "I AM WHO I AM" (Exod 3:14), and the difference is a helpful reminder of my place in this book. The first statement makes you laugh, and the second makes you tremble. My words may lead you to do either, but my life will surely not make you tremble. What I *yam* is a person in need of God's mercy; and I am also a person who thinks that there is a need for this book.

WHAT THIS BOOK IS NOT

There are good books available that describe in nonphilosophical terms the philosophy of ethics. These books deal with important questions about the definition of goodness and the complexities of decision making. They also deal with contemporary issues, applying biblical teachings to the problems in order to propose a Christian view. If this were such a book, you would expect to see, at the time that I write, chapters on AIDS, apartheid, and armament. However worthwhile such a book might be, it would require a well-trained philosopher and a knowledgeable analyst of current issues to write it. Many others are better qualified on both counts than I am.

I am trained as a theologian—more specifically, as an interpreter of the New Testament. Typically, a theologian will approach the subject of New Testament moral teaching by considering its starting point in the character of God, the differences between Jesus and Paul, or the tensions between present and future aspects of God's kingdom. These issues are particularly interesting to me, but not as the subject of this book. It may, however, help some readers to know what I will assume as a framework for the description that follows. I will assume that the reader is familiar with the basic Christian belief that God offers each person salvation by means of faith in his Son Jesus.[1] A life of service to God is the only possible expression of that faith. Doing good does not merit our salvation; rather, God's offer of salvation merits our doing good. Indeed, he provides the power (through his Spirit) for us to act in ways contrary to our fundamentally self-seeking natures. All of this can be affirmed without any particular denominational perspective, and the same can be said of all that follows.

This simple theological basis is ground enough for most feet to stand on. But it is likely that the demands that follow are enough for all feet to feel stepped on. It happens that I spend much of my time among theologically conservative

---

[1]If not, I recommend C. S. Lewis, *Mere Christianity* (New York: Macmillan, 1956), and J. I. Packer, *Knowing God* (Downers Grove, Ill.: InterVarsity, 1973), as two very helpful explanations of basic Christian belief.

Protestants, few of whom will be able to read this book without discomfort. I am also grateful to count as friends some earnest believers who are Roman Catholics, mainline Protestants, and charismatics, and they will all feel the same discomfort. That discomfort will be a holy discomfort if it unites us, not in theological details, but in a desire to live as people who are loved by God.

One important area of discussion that I neglect by design is social ethics. This will disappoint some readers, because the New Testament is seen increasingly as a document fundamentally concerned with social justice, with the plight of the world's poor and oppressed. But the fact is that New Testament writers lived in a world where organized social reform was not yet imagined and probably not possible. Implications and generalizations from personal ethics are certainly possible today, and they are essential. We should take part in good causes. Indeed, from the abolition of slavery to the abolition of gender discrimination, from public education to hospitals, most contemporary social movements and benefits can trace their roots directly to biblical ethics. But involvement in good causes does not constitute the goodness of the individual. The professed desire to change the world often masks insecurity about personal limitations. It is easier to direct attention toward distant or large-scale problems than to face personal problems. And it is easier to hate the unjust enemy than to love the victim. These dangers suggest that attention to large-scale problems, though necessary, is inadequate. There is something deeper, more basic, and logically prior to social transformation, and its description takes up most of the space of the New Testament. It is personal transformation. We must become loving people, one at a time, even while we may be working for the transformation of whole social systems.

A final exclusion has to do with popular lists of requirements and prohibitions commonly associated with

Christianity. This book is not a set of proof texts assembled from the Bible to affirm a current expression of morality. Unfortunately, the Bible has become for some a sort of doctor's house-call bag (complete with zippered black leather case) from which prescriptions are withdrawn to treat whatever "bug" is going around at the moment. Each generation has its own lists of expected "do's" and particularly nasty "don'ts," the observance of which signals to all observers: *this* is a *Christian*. Thus, for example, if I were writing in the mid-nineteenth century, I would include a chapter on Sabbath observance in which I would present biblical texts to prove that on Sundays, cooking and games are inappropriate, and that wearing dark-colored, formal attire is appropriate; I would state that Bible reading, works of charity, and serious conversation are to be the *exclusive* occupations of the day. A glimpse into the future would convince one of these people that millions of so-called Christians living in the late twentieth century do not deserve the name Christian when in their Sunday activities they blaspheme God and bow down to the standards of the world.

Lest the reader think that I am ridiculing the customs of the mid-nineteenth century, let me make it clear that I think I could build a stronger biblical case for Sabbath observance, Victorian style, than I could for many of the current expectations of Christian piety. The point is simply that the list of expectations,[2] which changes from time to time, does not always reflect the priorities of the Bible itself. Obviously,

[2]Perhaps I should not assume that the "list" is common knowledge: one should pray and read the Bible daily; attend church at least weekly; strive for the conversion of nonbelievers; give one-tenth of one's gross income (the "tithe") to a church; and avoid alcohol, tobacco, social dancing, gambling, pre- and extramarital sex, and bad language. The best book I have seen justifying this list is Carl H. Lundquist, *The Silent Issues of the Church* (Wheaton, Ill.: Victor Books, 1985). Charles Sheldon, *In His Steps*, is a classic of the early part of this century. Older than these (but best of all) is William Law, *A Serious Call to a Devout and Holy Life*.

to a group of people who consider the Bible to be the authoritative document for faith and practice, this is an odd state of affairs, perhaps even dangerous. Outsiders commonly misunderstand and equate the faith with the list of behavioral expectations. Christianity becomes, for them, a set of strange beliefs that one must suddenly feel convinced about and a set of enjoyable activities that one must suddenly stop enjoying. Neither set has any apparent logical relation to the other, unless it is that God wants us all to be as uncomfortable as possible—in mind *and* body. The stumbling block to belief today is not, as in the first century, the "foolishness of the cross" (1 Cor 1:21–25) so much as the foolishness of Christians.

Now, it will distress readers who are applauding at this point to learn that I approve and practice the behaviors on the current "list." Even though they seem arbitrary and culturally relative, I consider them quite sensible. But I do not consider them quite biblical. Or to put it another way, it does not appear that the Bible makes them out to be particularly important as signals of a transformed life.

WHAT THIS BOOK IS ABOUT

Books about ethics, books about theology, and books about social or behavioral issues all freely use the specific terminology of loving conduct: people ought to be humble, joyful, unified, sympathetic, and so forth. But these books seldom if ever stop to explain just what is meant by "humility" or "joy" or "unity" or "sympathy," much less their relation to each other or to Christian beliefs. Some commentaries on individual books of the Bible take up a particular behavior where it occurs in the text, and a thorough search of the best commentaries can be very fruitful *if* one has a clear idea of the passages and words to look for. But even then the basket of gathered fruit might benefit from some arrangement, and how should that be done? One key question this book attempts to answer is this: *What are the priorities and explanations of the New Testament itself about how followers of Jesus Christ ought to act in expressing their belief?* In other words, instead of asking what we should do in response to particular moral dilemmas or what we should do in response to certain theological problems, we should ask what we should do if we happen to wake up tomorrow morning.

The answer in general terms was given by Jesus when he said that we are to love God and our neighbors (Mark 12:28–35), particularly our fellow believers (John 13:34–35). That general command provides a logical sequence for this book: the relation to God, to fellow believers, and to others. The task is then to select and explain the specific expressions of love that are dominant in the New Testament.[3] These choices form the basis for the chapters of the book. When I use the word *dominant*, I disguise a somewhat complex process of judging importance. Repetition of words and their synonyms is certainly one simple way to ascertain importance, but it is not helpful in determining priorities or connections to other themes. At times the placement of a word in a passage or the placement of a passage in a book is a good indication of importance, and at times a single lengthy explanation of one behavior shows its relative priority over another that is mentioned in numerous lists of behaviors.

But while the process of sorting and explaining is more complex than I had guessed it would be, the result is more— I can only write *beautiful*—than I imagined it could be. A

---

[3] The Old Testament is assumed, not ignored, throughout, and Old Testament themes and texts will be drawn in where they help to give a fuller picture of a particular behavior. By their own selection and omission of Old Testament ethical material, New Testament authors give a good indication of those elements which are applicable in a Christian context. Therefore, although concentration on the New Testament involves some loss of detail and of historical richness, it would not be unfair to call it a *biblical* Christian view of loving conduct.

good botanist can increase our appreciation of all flowers when he dissects one to illustrate his delight at the complexity of its inner workings. A bad botanist, who merely cuts and classifies, reduces a flower to a *thing with parts*. I want to be a good botanist. What has grown in me as I have worked, and what I hope to communicate, is an image of biblical ethics as a dance in which each movement flows gracefully and logically from the one before. I should have seen this long ago, because I understood something of the music (which is theology), but I am dull, and, of course, in my crowd, dancing is something that *one does not do*. May the Composer and Choreographer have an easier time with you.

THE TENSION BETWEEN DEMAND AND MERCY

The hardest part of reading (or writing) this book is the constant reminder of human inadequacy. What follows are almost two hundred pages of explanations of things that one *ought to do*. This should drive the conscientious reader to despair and the sensible reader to some other book. But for the stalwart I offer an explanation in order to make the tension more manageable.

In different periods of history people have reacted differently to the problem that in Christianity people are told to be good and are also told that they are forgiven for not being good. My observation is that our own generation errs on the side of moral leniency: if one is theologically correct, believing in God's mercy, one's level of obedience is, well, largely optional. In other times, the reverse was true: doing the right things was the key, and only experts would pronounce God's mercy or discuss theology. The difficulty is to do both, to hold in constant tension God's seemingly impossible demands ("You, therefore, must be perfect" [Matt 5:48 RSV]) and his seemingly limitless mercy ("There is therefore now no condemnation for those who are in Christ

Jesus" [Rom 8:1 RSV]). Either these two truths contradict each other, or one is only an illusion, or they must both be taken very seriously. The first option is hardly possible because the same figures (Jesus, Paul, John, and others) affirm both, sometimes in adjacent paragraphs. The second option results either in pride ("There is no forgiveness: we have earned God's favor") or immorality ("There is no demand: we can do as we like"). Unless, of course, people are naturally good. But it is probably safe to assume that anyone who even picks up this book, let alone reads this far, has no illusions about being *naturally good,* or at the very least wants to be considerably better. So I will not argue the point.

What I will suggest for consideration is the following maxim: the extent of God's mercy is precisely that required to fill the space between what you ought to do and what you do. Both the demands and the mercy are tailored for the individual, so that no one can say, "I have done enough," much less, "My neighbor has not done enough." It may be a greater act of obedience for a child molester to abstain from one opportunity to molest than for a great evangelist to preach an effective sermon. To say that one person is "good" or "better than another" only reveals the limited perspective of the human observer. Thus Jesus pronounces forgiveness to a prostitute who cleans his feet while she receives abuse from the "good" people watching (Luke 7:36–50). What kind of God is this who congratulates bad people for doing small things and requires good people to do big things? Certainly not the one that most of us have created for ourselves. In answer to the question, "How much good must I do?" his answer is always, "More." In answer to the question, "Must I be better than that person is?" he replies, "You must be better than you are." He does not look at the point that I have reached on some Objective Moral Scale, or even at the amount of progress I have made since beginning my homeward journey. Instead, he looks at me, only me, and says, "Whatever good you do makes me glad, but no amount of good that you do satisfies me. Still, I *am* satisfied, not by your love but by my own love—by giving from myself what you would not give."

THE ETHIC OF STRIVING

For me, then, to refuse to participate, or to claim attainment on a scale of my own invention or on a scale of current societal expectation would be to say, "No, thank you. The offer of mercy is all very nice, but I would prefer more of a bargain, where I perform to my (minimal) expectations and you forgive the difference." You see how this misses the whole point of the offer of mercy: it is stupid, and, worse, it is presumptuous. The only honest response to this offer of God, the only response that takes it seriously, is one that puts into action the words, "Help me, then, to make you glad, *to narrow the gap that your mercy fills.*"

The point is not to arrive but to strive. I have attempted to explain this without reference to particular biblical passages for the sake of those who are unfamiliar (or perhaps too familiar) with biblical language, but it is important to understand that the idea is not new. It appears between the lines and in the lines throughout the New Testament. The most thorough statement of this "ethic of striving" is made by Paul, who follows a discussion of righteousness with these words:

> Not that I have already obtained all this, or have already been made perfect, but I press on to take hold of that for which Christ Jesus took hold of me. Brothers, I do not consider myself yet to have taken hold of it. But one thing I do: Forgetting what is behind and straining toward what is ahead, I press on toward the goal to win the prize for which God has called me heavenward in Christ Jesus (Phil 3:12–14).

In his next sentence Paul sums up: "Let those who are perfect have this outlook, and if anyone has a different outlook, God will surely make that clear to you."⁴ It is this way of living, then, not any level or quantity of goodness, that Paul considers perfection. But this is not the only explicit New Testament passage that teaches this. Paul uses the word "strive" when describing his own work in Colossians 1:28–29 and 1 Timothy 4:8–10, and when recommending mutual upbuilding to others (1 Cor 14:12; cf. Rom 2:7). Hebrews 4:12 and 12:14 speak of striving for goodness. And Jesus, of course, again and again, promises satisfaction for those whose lives show that they "seek first God's kingdom and his righteousness" (Matt 6:33; cf. 7:7; Luke 13:24). Jesus recognized that most people simply want to have a good time pleasing themselves, ignoring God's demands and his mercy: they are in great danger (Luke 17:26–29). The Pharisees, on the other hand, had stopped striving because they, being very good, apparently thought they had arrived, and we must do better than that, according to Jesus (Matt 5:20). We must, in fact, be perfect (v. 48). This does not mean that we must be without fault but that we must take equally seriously both the demand and the mercy. We can never be content with ourselves, but we can ever be content with God.

FOR FUTURE REFERENCE

The point where demand and mercy meet varies for each person. I will not make reference to this "ethic of striving" often in the pages that follow. Instead, I will simply ask you

---

⁴I would propose such a translation as preferable to that of the NIV, which reads "mature" instead of "perfect." The same Greek word lies behind "Be perfect, therefore, as your heavenly Father is perfect" (Matt 5:48), and "mature" seems to be a rather weak word to use for God. We do better to change our understanding in conformity to the words than to change the words in conformity to our understanding.

to make reference to it whenever, beneath the weight of obligation, you are tempted to despair, and *especially* when you are tempted to be complacent.

Part I

The Believer in Relation to God

Love the Lord your God with all your heart,
with all your soul and with all your mind.
This is the first and greatest commandment.

Matthew 22:37–38

• 1 •

Humility:

"Blessed Are the Poor in Spirit"

The following scene occurs only rarely outside of Hollywood. There, horribly, it is termed "entertainment." But here, this time, in order to grasp a concept essential to what follows, you must imagine yourself as the primary player in the drama. This time, the story is not on the screen but in the mirror.

It is late at night, and the house is empty. You have arranged for the room to be dimly lit, almost dark. You met a stranger a few hours ago, and that person is here with you now. Just the two of you, nervous and tentative, and your desire. The choices that led up to this moment were only half-conscious—an attraction, some tentative flirtation, an easy arrangement of time and place. And now this. The details have fallen into place so that there are no strings attached, no chance of discovery, no responsibility later. Wrong, perhaps; but easy, definitely. And now the wanting has joined with the dark. The kisses and caresses are hesitant at first, self-conscious. But they become easier and more eager until desire swells like a wave and carries away consciousness of everything but itself. In another moment the passion crests. . . .

And then there is the click of the doorknob turning.

A flood of terrible light intrudes as an unsuspecting hand touches the wall switch. And there in the doorway stands the one person in this world who would be most hurt by the sight. The expression on that beloved face is not anger, not confusion—to those perhaps you could respond—but pain. Terrible pain that can only be seen in the instant when suddenly an innocent trust is betrayed, a precious gift is trampled, a tender love is ridiculed by the beloved. There is no place for you to hide. There is no explanation to make. You are reduced in that moment to complete shame, to pure need.

The scene is painful to imagine, and it is no less painful to bring it from the realm of imagination to the reality of our own behavior. For there is no sheet to pull over myself, no possibility of protesting that this scene is not part of my particular repertoire of wrongdoing. If I have not done this, I have desired it. And if I have not desired it, I have done or desired something equally bad. And even if I have no such evil deeds to name, the sum of all my petty little wrongs is far greater than any one vile scene that I can remember or imagine. So the scene need not correspond to a particular moment in my history. It serves just as well as a substitution or a condensation of other moments. But the worst pain of all is that when the door swings open and the glaring light exposes my behavior, the face framed in the doorway is far more innocent, and thus far more pained, than that of any human loved one. The trust betrayed, the gift trampled, the love ridiculed—they are from God himself. He entrusted me with freedom, he gave me a life of opportunity, he taught me what love is like. But I have been unfaithful.

The moment that one is faced with one's own essential badness is an awful moment, but it is also a precious moment. For if in that instant a person is reduced, it is not a reduction from the normal to something abnormal, but a reduction to true humanness. At that point of discovery all the façades are torn away, no games of self-justification are being played, one's voice is not whimpering, "I'm not as bad as some" or "I do a lot of good, too." At that moment the safe, obscuring fog clears from the mirror, and then it turns out not to be a mirror at all but a window. And Someone on the other side has seen all. It is the moment of basic contact between an honest creature and the Creator: what I described in the scene above as a reduction to pure need. To be found a desperately needy creature is to be, in the words of Jesus, *poor in spirit*.

It is fitting that the first words of Jesus' first recorded sermon are "Blessed are the poor in spirit" (Matt 5:3). The words contain a demand and provide a hope. Here, indeed, is what many readers of the four gospels are often disappointed not to find easily amid all of Jesus' moral teachings: the gospel within the Gospels. Only the person who will acknowledge a desperate need of God will accrue the blessing, and only by beginning in this manner will the rest of the demands of Jesus be met. In *The Pilgrim's Progress*, John Bunyan provides a memorable picture of a man who, once realizing his need and the source of its fulfillment, begins to run frantically in the right direction screaming "Eternal life! Eternal life!" What an unseemly public display, the neighbors say. But honesty will produce desperation, and suddenly it does not matter what the neighbors will think but only what God will provide. Jesus, with a typical twist, promises that to the poor in spirit God will give the entire kingdom of heaven: the one whose self-perception is that of one truly undeserving becomes the recipient of the one thing that is truly overwhelming.

SPIRITUAL AND ECONOMIC POVERTY

The economic connotation of this first Beatitude is often stressed, especially when one reads that in a similar sermon in

Luke, Jesus says simply, "Blessed are you poor." Matthew may have added "in spirit" for clarification, but he did not thereby "spiritualize" the statement. Both "poor" and "poor in spirit" are legitimate Greek renderings by the gospel writers of the Aramaic word that Jesus used. In the Old Testament this word is often translated "afflicted" or "humbled" and refers to both material and spiritual need (e.g., Pss 35:13; 70:5; Isa 58:3). The one who lacks material provision cries out to God for deliverance, but the deliverance may not come in the form of earthly riches (e.g., Mary in Luke 1:46–56). Conversely, a wealthy king like David cries to God for help and describes himself as poor and needy (Ps 40:17). The common denominator is desperate need and acknowledgment that only God can meet that need. Our English word "poor" allows a similar overlapping: if a man loses his wife suddenly in an automobile accident, we do not hesitate to exclaim, "The poor man!" even if he is a millionaire. He is a man with a great need.

Synonymous with the command to be poor in spirit, and dominant in the New Testament, is the familiar admonition "Humble yourself." Jesus made the meaning clear by telling the story of a Pharisee and a tax collector:

> Two men went up to the temple to pray, one a Pharisee and the other a tax collector. The Pharisee stood up and prayed about himself: "God, I thank you that I am not like other men— robbers, evildoers, adulterers—or even like this tax collector. I fast twice a week and give a tenth of all I get." But the tax collector stood at a distance. He would not even look up to heaven, but beat his breast and said, "God, have mercy on me, a sinner." I tell you that this man, rather than the other, went home justified before God. For everyone who exalts himself will be humbled, and he who humbles himself will be exalted. (Luke 18:10–14)

Note that the tax collector did not manufacture a self-demeaning attitude; he simply told God what he was. It is the self-justification of the Pharisee that is the distortion. Humility is not lowering; rather, pride is illegitimate elevation. Humility is mere honesty. Note too that the humble man's confession is not comparative: he refers to himself simply as a sinner (*"the"* sinner, NASB). To inform God that he is one among many, or that he is worse than another, or even that he is worse than he used to be, would be a step away from responsibility. Instead, he is conscious only of his place before God: that of a creature in need of mercy, mercy that only God can supply.

A quick scan of the Gospels will reveal this theme on almost every page. At times it appears as a simple formula: "Whoever humbles himself will be exalted" (Matt 23:12; Luke 14:11), or "The last will be first" (Matt 20:16; Luke 13:30). At other times it is more subtle, as for example when the disciples acknowledged that they could do nothing *but* follow Jesus (John 6:68). Again and again the Gospels present people who know desperate need, and they present God's Son as the one who meets it. The theme continues throughout the New Testament. Paul reckons everything that he ever had or was as "refuse" next to the knowledge of God's salvation (Phil 3:8). For him, glorification comes only from his Lord (Gal 6:14). James 4:10 commands believers, "Humble yourselves before the Lord and he will lift you up." Peter in 1 Peter 5:6 enjoins disciples, "Humble yourselves, therefore, under God's mighty hand, that he may lift you up in due time." Alcoholics Anonymous and related programs have long stressed that successful rehabilitation must begin at "rock bottom": the first step up is to admit one's own inadequacy and the need for help. This principle is no less true with regard to substances other than alcohol. Someone else may be controlled by food or work or sex or money or leisure, and that person will use the same methods of denial as the alcoholic: "I can control this, I can give it up any time, I can fix myself if I ever need to—and I don't need to right now, thank you."

Even more common than denial is imaginary conquest: to turn conversations to criticism of events, ideas, and people, or to one's own activities and opinions. Ah, how much neater, smaller, and controllable the world seems when one is at its center, trusting in one's own basic goodness and understanding. And thus subconsciously we try to convince others so that we ourselves might be more convinced. We are like fat spiders who scurry to poison and wrap neatly each new event or idea or person landing in our web and then return to the center to chortle over our accomplishment to a companion— until the time when even that person becomes a victim. And then, in moments of solitude, we can return in thought to feed on these conquests.

Is this predatory image too harsh a view of human conduct? Certainly popular literature, education, and even preaching will avoid or deny it. But just as certainly, a careful inventory of the thoughts and activities of the past few hours will confirm it. A moment of honesty will stand against all the persuasion that supports self-justification. Paul, with great candor, describes in the first person the frustration of moral inadequacy, which when addressed to God is the moment of humility:

> So I find this law at work: When I want to do good, evil is right there with me. For in my inner being I delight in God's law; but I see another law at work in the members of my body, waging war against the law of my mind and making me a prisoner of the law of sin at work within my members. What a wretched man I am! Who will rescue me from this body of death? (Rom 7:21–24)

The spider's venom has infected the spider, and what was meant to control the spider's world has turned to corruption.

The body will not conquer—it will not even live—and the spider is alone, and afraid.

FEAR OF GOD

What is this fear that occurs at the moment of humility before God? "The fear of the LORD is the beginning of wisdom," says Proverbs 9:10, but in our lack of wisdom we prefer to redefine fear. The experience might be defined in a dictionary as "anticipation of harm." A biblical writer put it more bluntly: "Fear has to do with punishment" (1 John 4:18). This concept grates against our independent spirits and our notions of God as all-providing and all-forgiving. After all, we love God, and does not 1 John 4:18 also affirm that perfect love casts out all fear? Yes. But when the door swings open and the light fills the room, how perfect is the love that is revealed lying there?

To the extent that our love is not perfect love, there is cause for fear. Fear of God is defined in several ways so as to take the sting out of the experience, or to excuse missing the experience. One way is to define fear as "honor" or "respect": we should give God his due, take him seriously, revere him. Another way is to define fear as "awe": God is grand, he is incredible, and we should stand in wonder at his greatness. Both of these are legitimate responses to God, but they are not synonymous with fear when they are used by New Testament authors. To "honor" in the New Testament is to follow protocol, to give what is due to another person by virtue of position; the word is used with parents (Matt 15:4; Eph 6:2) and rulers (Rom 13:7; 1 Peter 2:17) as well as God (Matt 15:8; Phil 1:20 RSV) as object. Fear, on the other hand, is due in the New Testament only to God, and in 1 Peter 2:17 this is set in *contrast* to the honor due to human rulers. To be in "awe" in the New Testament is to marvel. This is a spontaneous response primarily to God's activity, usually to a demonstration of benevolent power. There is normally an element of surprise, as when the disciples marvel at the healing powers of Jesus (Matt 8:27; Mark 5:20). Fear, on the other hand, is a reaction to potential harm. When, for example, the disciples "cried out in fear" (Matt 14:26) when they saw Jesus walking toward them on the water, their fear hardly consisted of wonder at God's goodness: according to the text, "they were terrified." They anticipated harm. The assumption was and still is that other-worldly beings are unfriendly or in some way dangerous. As one who presumably has the will and the power to punish human wrongdoing, God is likely to be the most dangerous of all. This is the sense of numerous New Testament commands, among them 1 Peter 1:17: "Since you call on a Father who judges each man's work impartially, live your lives as strangers here in reverent *fear*" (cf. Luke 12:5; Rom 11:20; 2 Cor 5:11; Col 3:22; Heb 2:15).

Fear, then, is anticipation of harm as a result of God's evaluation. Respect and awe are also due to God, but in situations other than the moment of humility. It could be said that we respect God when we talk about him, we are in awe when we think about his works, but we fear when we *face him*. Polite abstraction is swept away in that moment: "Then I turned to see the voice that was speaking to me, and . . . when I saw him, I fell at his feet as though dead" (Rev 1: 12, 17 RSV; cf. Job 42:5–6).

BETWEEN GUILT AND COMFORT

Passages that require that the believer in some sense live in fear, humility, or in poverty of spirit appear to create a conflict with passages that assure salvation. Why dread the consequences of my conduct if God loves me and forgives me? Or why experience fear as an ongoing activity when a one-time repentance is all that is necessary to assure salvation?

The answer to this question is of fundamental importance: it will determine how one walks the narrow path between pathological guilt on the one hand and blind moral complacency on the other. The latter is more common because it affirms the desire for self-justification and because it is easy to list a few biblical texts about Christ's once-for-all sacrifice. But in reality, it is a variation on an old theme, one that Paul encountered in the slogan "Let us continue in sin that grace may abound!" (Rom 6:1, 15). Paul opposed this notion vehemently.

The New Testament makes it clear that only a lifetime of obedience demonstrates the validity of one's initial commitment to the lordship of Christ (see, e.g., Mark 13:13; Luke 8:15; Col 1:22–23; Heb 10:36; 2 Peter 1:10). This is not to deny the doctrine of "eternal security." Those who teach this doctrine acknowledge that one who initially shows every evidence of sincere faith may eventually fail to persevere; and therefore to prove not to have been saved in the first place. But while Scripture necessitates obedience, it does not teach that one loses forgiveness for every new sin following conversion: the danger is of a pattern of disobedience (Heb 3:12–15). The danger in our day is of a mere theological claim to salvation: "I prayed this prayer"; "I believe God forgives me"; "I have a relationship with Jesus." These statements may be true, but according to the New Testament (Matt 7:21–27; James 2:14–26), they are not grounds for salvation. Obedience is the ground upon which assurance stands solidly (2 Tim 4:7–8).

Well, then, how bad can I get before I am in danger? A very natural question, which the New Testament refuses to answer. For if the New Testament were to draw such a line, we would busy ourselves describing how close we can walk to it without stepping over it. We could become worse than the Pharisees. The alternative is to take the demand of complete obedience just as seriously as the offer of complete forgiveness—to find a harmony between guilt and comfort rather than to make one or the other meaningless. Jesus called it a narrow road. It may be a razor's edge, a high wire.

There remains, therefore, ample ground for fear. As love grows, fear lessens, but regular reflection on one's conduct will effectively prevent complacency. There is a confidence that is not cocky. It is a confidence in the quality of God's love for me, not mine for him.

THE CONNECTING THREAD

It is the love of God that elevates all of this from a list of statements about the Bible to an interconnected whole about life as we live it. There is nothing more important than to grasp—or, more accurately, to be grasped by—that love. If we are to be personally transformed, it must be a Person who does it.

In the introduction I compared biblical ethics to a dance. It could also be compared to a tapestry. It is possible to stand back and appreciate the whole tapestry, and it is possible to focus on any one of many scenes. But what is most remarkable about this tapestry, and what is revealed only by close scrutiny, is that the threads can all be traced to one scene at the center of the whole. If that scene were removed, the rest could not be understood, and the whole tapestry would unravel.

The figure in the central scene, the source from which all of the threads emanate, is Jesus. In terms of this particular chapter, the tapestry portrays him hanging from a cross, his eyes open, clear, and in pain, at the moment that he cries out in despair (Mark 15:34). That is a moment in history, but the thread moves out through the tapestry and out from the tapestry and into your life and mine. And then, at another moment in your history or mine, that cry of dereliction is the face in the doorway. The pain is not now nor ever was pain at his own separation from God. It is clear-eyed, conscious agony that the one he so loves—me—has betrayed him. But because this was and is God's expression of love, the moment is not lost, the thread does not end in a dark void. It is in fact this moment of greatest wrong that he makes into the greatest right. He conquers pain by knowing it, in person. Who could have ever imagined a humble God, a God who would choose to make of his human end our eternal beginning? We would not know humility unless he had known it first.

· 2 ·

Joy:
"Rejoice in the Lord"

What is it to be happy? We tend to define the word by imagining an experience that *produces* happiness: "Happiness is listening to Mozart." Or we describe reasons to be happy: "Happiness is being approved by my peers." But such statements do not describe the sensation of happiness. It is worthwhile to focus, at least for a moment, on the experience itself in order to insure that we are thinking *about* it and not *around* it.

When a person is happy, a physical sensation of movement, perhaps an illusion of expansion, occurs within the chest cavity. Then a kind of ripple effect sends the sensation outward and produces a smile or a laugh or a wriggling movement in the arms and legs. At some point the person becomes conscious of the sensation and reflects, "This is good; I am happy."

Why do we seek this experience? It is certainly an unusual—we might even say unnatural—physical state. And in terms of frequency and duration, we must admit that it is a rare experience. It seems strange to talk about it as much as we do, as if it were a common occurence or expectation.

When we claim that everyone should possess as an inalienable right "the pursuit of happiness," we may possibly imagine a figure running toward an attractive house or some other material object. In other words, we envision only the objects that many mistakenly think will *produce* happiness. And we entertain ourselves much more with craving than with having. We might better, therefore, refer to the cherished right as "the happiness of *pursuit*." The thrill of *desire* is more constant and more characteristic of human life than the experience of happiness.

Perhaps, then, a better explanation of our desire for the experience of happiness is that in the moment of happiness, desire is *set aside*. Or, to put it positively, the words "I am happy" could be replaced by the words "I am satisfied." A new question then arises. How can anyone ever say, "I am satisfied"? Am I not always inadequate before God? Is there not always pain in my life? Are not people starving somewhere? *Is not happiness therefore a lie?* Is not happiness rare because we can manage to delude ourselves only briefly before we return to craving? Certainly not. And this is the crucial point in understanding the abundant New Testament material on the subject. The essence of satisfaction, and therefore the essence of happiness, is not to say that all is good, but that all is part of a greater good. Contentment, then, is ultimately contentment with God, or it can never go deeper than pain or last longer than the moment before sober reflection.

HAPPINESS AND JOY

Someone may object to this explanation, saying that it unneccessarily spiritualizes common human experiences like family gatherings, laughter among friends, and personal pleasures that we normally associate with the word *happiness*. Should we not leave "happiness" out of the discussion and speak of "joy" to denote satisfaction in the spiritual realm? It is common to make such a distinction. But to do so is unwarranted by the biblical vocabulary, and it creates a false distinction between "earthly" and "heavenly" satisfaction. Consider, for example, the descriptions of heaven in Revelation: a huge family gathers in a beautiful bright place, has plenty of food to eat together, and enjoys a great time without sickness or pain or death. The description is thoroughly physical. And then consider what people do who are filled with "spiritual" joy: they sing (Eph 5:19–20), they dance (Ps 149:3), they kiss (1 Peter 5:14), and they eat together (Acts 2:46–47). The physical cannot be separated from the spiritual, and the happiness produced by a mother's embrace, a friend's witty remark, a sunset, or a favorite song are all foretastes of heaven. Indeed, they are reminders that when God pronounced "It is good" over the world he had made and all the simple, human, physical joys that are part of it, he meant the words to last long beyond the Fall. Because we cannot hear the words now without shame over what we have done to the creation, we have a tendency to look beyond physical things. But the hope of heaven is that we will be able to say all-inclusively, without shame or qualification, what in this present life we can say only in fleeting moments: "This is good; I am happy."

The New Testament command to rejoice is oriented toward this future hope, but it is a reality that reaches back into the present to give comfort and courage in difficult situations. The Beatitudes (Matt 5:3–12) make this point very clearly. Jesus announces that people who exhibit certain characteristics are "blessed" (sometimes translated "happy") *now* because they will receive something later. Verses 11–12 are particularly instructive, because here the words "rejoice and be glad" in verse 12 are parallel with "Blessed are you" in verse 11. "Blessed," then, is defined by Jesus as having reason to celebrate now—in spite of appearances, because of promises. This understanding relieves the tension of verse 4 where, oddly enough, the person who *mourns* is *blessed*. The implied command is obviously not to be happy and sad simultaneously but rather to recognize now in these circumstances (present earthly deprivation) one's cause for joy (future heavenly provision). This message is a recurrent one in the New Testament. Paul rejoices in his sufferings (Col 1:24) and recommends the same to all believers who wish to communicate effectively their confidence in God (Phil 4:4–5). Peter, similarly, exhorts Christians, "Rejoice in so far as you share Christ's sufferings, that you may also rejoice and be glad when his glory is revealed" (1 Peter 4:13 RSV; cf. 1:6–9). It is precisely because God has the future in hand that the hurting believer can say, "This is not good in itself, but it is part of a greater good."

This experience of satisfaction is happiness, and the New Testament uses the same vocabulary for the experience in the midst of trial as it does for the experience in the midst of pleasant circumstances. The words *gladness* and *joy* are synonymous (e.g., Luke 1:14 RSV; 6:23) and describe what is more commonly called "happiness." There is nothing more "spiritual" about joy that distinguishes it from "mere" happiness. In other words, to affirm that God wants his children to have joy is to affirm that he wants them to be happy, to be satisfied.

THE CAUSE OF JOY

Since this satisfaction must involve more than an arbitrary gratification of desire, we are led naturally to ask, "What is the *content* of this happiness? What am I to be happy about?" And from that point we are led to another question: "How am I to express satisfaction? Practically speaking, how is joy initiated?"

In answer to the first question the New Testament gives

a clear and consistent answer: "Rejoice in your hope" (Rom 12:12 RSV; cf. Matt 5:12; Luke 10:20). Hope refers to the future promise and present benefit of God's mercy and love. One concise description is offered in Colossians 1:12–14, where believers are exhorted to live lives characterized by joy,

> giving thanks to the Father, who has qualified you to share in the inheritance of the saints in the kingdom of light. For he has rescued us from the dominion of darkness and brought us into the kingdom of the Son he loves, in whom we have redemption, the forgiveness of sins.

The contrast drawn here between darkness and light recalls the scene described in the previous chapter. It is the same light, but the one on whom it shines has changed. In the first flash, the light is painful: it reveals, it damns, with silent and terrible power. That is the moment of humility. But something amazing happens at precisely that point. Something that can be truly known only by one who understands that the face in the doorway is not that of one who is angered but that of one who is wounded. If he is God, he knows me completely before the moment the light comes on, and that must mean that he is *willingly* wounded. If he is *willingly* wounded, it must be that there is a purpose for that moment, and it must be that it is for my benefit, for him to express his love. . . . As thought follows thought, and each conclusion is seen to be a necessary conclusion, the moment of humility is transformed, and the light no longer gives pain. It gives clarity. It allows the first glimpses of what has been true all along and of what will be true in the end. Because of that, suddenly, there is joy in what is now. It is fitting, then, that the description of the heavenly city, the ultimate hope that reaches back into the present, includes the image of eternal light:

The city does not need the sun or the moon to shine on it, for the glory of God gives it light, and the Lamb is its lamp. The nations will walk by its light, and the kings of the earth will bring their splendor into it. On no day will its gates ever be shut, for there will be no night there. The glory and honor of the nations will be brought into it. . . . There will be no more night. They will not need the light of a lamp or the light of the sun, for the Lord God will give them light. And they will reign for ever and ever. (Rev 21:23–26; 22:5)

Can anyone imagine that scene, however imperfectly, without wanting it desperately? And can anyone who expects it not feel a thrill at the thought, "I will *be there!*" This is the *fact* that brings joy. The "how to" question naturally follows: What does one do to initiate joy?

WHAT JOY IS NOT

To begin to answer that question, it is necessary to distinguish the activity of rejoicing from two experiences related to it but not quite the same, according to biblical writers. The first is the experience of peace. One might equate this word with joy and explain, "I experience joy as a quiet, inner peace, the satisfaction built on a settled relationship with the Lord." This is indeed an adequate explanation of peace, but New Testament writers do not use "peace" and "joy" synonymously. At times the two words appear in the same verse (Rom 14:17; 15:13; Gal 5:22) but not to define each other. "Peace" is common in both Testaments, and as a term for relations between God and man it is most closely related to the idea of *security*. Thus Jesus promises in John 14:27: "Peace I leave with you; my peace I give you. I do not give to you as the world gives. Do not let your hearts be troubled and do not be afraid." (cf. Rom 16:20; 1 Thess 5:23; Heb 13:20.) Peace, then, is the conviction that God is providing and will provide what is necessary for salvation—

in spite of threats from within or without. It is initiated by God: there is no command to "be peaceful" like that to "rejoice." Rather, peace is the primary *reason* to rejoice. Thus, when Paul communicates his desire that the peace of God, which transcends all understanding, will guard the believers' hearts and minds in Christ Jesus (Phil 4:7), he does not mean by "transcends all understanding" that peace is happiness too wonderful for words to express. He writes these words immediately following a statement of assurance in the midst of a trying situation (vv. 4–6). God's peace, which "transcends all understanding," then, is security in circumstances that naturally promote insecurity. Joy follows peace, but it is not peace.

Another experience often equated with the biblical notion of joy has been described by C. S. Lewis. In the experience of Lewis (and many others), there are fleeting moments of intense longing and—just as fleeting—satisfaction of that longing. These are glimpses of heaven, when the fully human desire for God is met for an instant by God's presence. The setting varies from person to person. For Lewis it was, on one occasion, the sight of distant hills, on another a favorite piece of music, on another an illustration in a book. The search for the source of these experiences, which he called "joy," led him ultimately to Christianity. Since both the longing and its satisfaction point to something outside normal human experience, he reasoned, they are not likely to be manufactured, and they must be some sort of message of attraction sent by God.

However true this may be, it is unfortunate that Lewis was not able to find a word other than "joy" for the experience he described so clearly. For although there are a few instances where we might argue that a biblical author is expressing what Lewis described, Lewis' definition of joy is too narrow to apply to most New Testament references. The phenomenon he describes is very rare in human experience, and it is properly regarded as a gift from God, given according to God's discretion at particular times. If this is joy, how can one "rejoice . . . always" (Phil 4:4; 1 Thess 5:16), or what word can we use for less intense but equally real experiences of happiness? Lewis described something very real and very important, but it is not identical to joy as the biblical writers understood it.

PRODUCING JOY

With a more clear idea of what joy is not, we can begin to approach a more precise and positive definition. To begin, it must be stressed that the activity of joy assumes an understanding. In other words, joy is a response, the activity that follows reflection. Joy cannot be separated from the fact that produces it, the fact of God's gift of peace, his gift of light.

The production of joy is sometimes attempted in churches by the manipulation of emotions through stirring music, touching anecdotes, or physical contact. This is not the joy born of hope that the New Testament describes and commands. Joy produced by the senses is just that, and it would be manufactured in churches with less confusion if worshipers were simply given hot fudge sundaes. No doubt many would partake with great thanksgiving, but they would not depart thinking that they had been obedient to the command to rejoice. Those who rejoice do not merely *feel* something wonderful that leads them to knowledge; rather, they *know* something wonderful that leads them to joy.

JOY IN ACTION

What, then, of the activity of rejoicing? Both because the New Testament mentions joy often without describing it and because the New Testament assumes much of the Old, we will get a fuller picture by giving some attention to the psalms and prophets.

The most characteristic expression of joy, occurring scores of times in Old Testament poetry, is a shout: "Rejoice in the LORD and be glad, you righteous; sing, all you who are upright in heart!" (Ps 32:11; cf. Ezra 3:11–13; Isa 42:11). The words translated "shout" are also used for the battle cry of an army. As an expression of joy, a shout is spontaneous and inarticulate, and as such it is altogether genuine. What could be more innocent—and contagious—than a sudden cry of delight from a happy child? How can I help but smile when my toddler shouts with glee when her favorite toy—her father—enters the room? It is to this image that Paul refers when he wants to communicate the joy of discovering that God is the Father of each believer: "When we cry, 'Abba! Father!' it is the Spirit himself bearing witness with our spirit that we are children of God" (Rom 8:15–16 RSV; cf. Gal 4:6).

Singing, not surprisingly, is another common way to express joy. Since a shout is often followed by a song, it is common to see the words together in the Old Testament: "Shout aloud and sing for joy, people of Zion, for great is the Holy One of Israel among you" (Isa 12:6; cf. Pss 65:13; 71:23). Words of praise set to music can give full and articulate expression to joy. Such songs channel the feeling that bursts forth from a knowledge of God's goodness. Songs do not stifle my feeling but direct it toward God and toward my neighbor. For when the rush of emotion is played out, God and my neighbor will still be there. Without such direction for joyful expression, our tendency is to desire repetition of the experience. We want to *feel* it again and again, and the experience or the longing for it becomes something like a drug. The end result is a turning in on oneself—the ultimate idol to worship, the ultimate alternative to the love of God.

The New Testament continues the Old Testament

emphasis on song, admonishing those who are filled with God's Spirit to "address one another in psalms and hymns and spiritual songs" (Eph 5:19 RSV; cf. Col 3:16; James 5:13). This threefold division corresponds to contemporary alternatives. "Psalms" are Scripture passages set to music (such as the Old Testament psalms or their New Testament equivalents; e.g., Luke 1:46–55, 68–79). "Hymns" are original compositions, and there is strong evidence that New Testament examples include Eph 5:14; Phil 2:6–11; 1 Tim 3:16, and Rev 4:8. "Spiritual songs" were probably the ancient equivalent of choruses: shorter quotations or phrases in scriptural language expressing truths of the faith.

The contents of these songs are invariably declarations of God's greatness. One interesting feature that often characterizes Old Testament psalms is the inclusion of nature in the expression of joy. Dawn and sunset (Ps 65:8), sun, moon, and stars (148:3), forests (96:12), mountains (98:8), seas (96:11), even animals (148:10) join the "singing." All of these join with human beings to give praise to God for his greatness. Although this cannot be construed fairly as "environmental awareness" in the modern sense, it does communicate the unity and importance of all creation. If the rivers (Ps 98:8) and trees (Isa 55:12) are to "clap their hands in joy," the humble but significant duty falls to us to insure that those hands are *clean*.

Closely related to singing as an expression of joy are the use of musical instruments and, more rarely, the activity of dancing. Psalm 150 is a good example because it leads from statements of the *reasons* for expressing joy to recommendations about the *method*. In other words, one does not make music or dance in order to produce joy; rather, one knows joy and then expresses it by means of music or dance (cf. 2 Sam 6:14–16; Ps 30:11; 71:22; Rev 5:8):

Praise the LORD.
Praise God in his sanctuary;
    praise him in his mighty heavens.
Praise him for his acts of power;
    praise him for his surpassing greatness.
Praise him with the sounding of the trumpet,
    praise him with the harp and lyre,
Praise him with tambourine and dancing,
    praise him with strings and flute.
Praise him with the clash of cymbals
    praise him with resounding cymbals.
Let everything that has breath praise the LORD.
Praise the LORD.

One important form of expression often found in the New Testament is the demonstration of joy in prose. Even across the barriers of time, culture, and language, one cannot fail to recognize the joy of Paul in certain passages. When, for example, he reaches the end of the first thorough, systematic explanation of Christian doctrine ever written, he concludes:

> No, in all these things we are more than conquerors through him who loved us. For I am convinced that neither death nor life, neither angels nor demons, neither the present nor the future, nor any powers, neither height nor depth, nor anything else in all creation, will be able to separate us from the love of God that is in Christ Jesus our Lord. (Rom 8:37–39)

Mere knowledge would write simply, "Nothing can separate us . . . ," but joy demands a list. Nor is this unusual for Paul. Three chapters later, he concludes another delicate and thorough explanation by exclaiming: "Oh, the depth of the riches of the wisdom and knowledge of God! How unsearchable his judgments and his paths beyond tracing out!" (Rom 11:33).

This pattern can be observed again and again in New Testament doctrinal explanations (see, e.g., 1 Cor 15:51–57; 2 Cor 2:14; Jude 24–25). To these writers, the proclamation of truth was not simply a matter of precise explanations or the correction of opposing views. It was a matter of the heart. God reached through their minds to stir them by the truth of their own words, and now and then in reading their letters we are the grateful recipients of their resulting expressions of joy.

PUBLIC AND PRIVATE EXPRESSION

We should not conclude a consideration of joy without addressing the question of personal style. To what extent must I externalize my joy?

The fact that the Scriptures do not explicitly answer this question offers encouragement for all. Shouting, singing, dancing, and other expressions of joy can all be done privately, in groups, or before groups. Examples of different styles appear throughout the Bible. People with different personalities, therefore, should feel no compulsion to conform to any one model of joyfulness. Many admire—and out of frustrated emulation, often come to resent—the perpetual smiler who is always ready with words of joy. In most cases such a person would wear the same natural smile, without good cause, even if he or she were an atheist. One who is naturally sober or quiet should not assume, however, that an effusive person is shallow or stupid. Nor should that reserved person feel pressure to conform, to publicize joy. The same David who danced naked for joy before God and all the people (2 Sam 6) also wrote these words:

> My soul will be satisfied as with the richest
>   of foods;
> with singing lips my mouth will praise you.
>
> On my bed I remember you;
>   I think of you through the watches of the night
>   (Ps 63:5–6; cf. 4:4; 77:6).

The activity of rejoicing will vary according to the person and the situation. Indeed, one cause for rejoicing is the wonderful variety of ways to rejoice. What could be more generous, what could be more simple, what could be more inclusive, what could be more innocent, what could be more exuberant, what could be more *satisfying*, than the last two sentences of the Book of Psalms?

> Let everything that has breath praise the LORD!
> Praise the LORD!

• 3 •

Prayer:

"Pray Without Ceasing"

Prayer is talking to God. Simple enough. Why is it so difficult to do? There are a number of good reasons, and until we face them honestly, we cannot move toward good prayer. One problem is that we cannot see God as we can most of what fills our lives. Spouses and potential purchases and disagreeable neighbors come to us continually and demand our attention. But God remains invisible and leaves us to take the initiative. It is not natural to pay attention to something that we cannot see, even out of a sense of obligation. Of course, we pay great attention to the as-yet unseen objects of our greed, lust, and ambition, but at least they *would be* visible if we attained them. And so we think about them frequently.

And yet . . .

John wrote that the one who longs for God will be pure and will see him (1 John 3:1–3), and Jesus himself said that the pure in heart will see God (Matt 5:8). Longing for *this* unseen object will result in the attainment of something visible. What then of my usual longings? Terrible thought: my daydreams are the true measure of my heart, my true longings, *my real prayers*. So prayer is not after all a matter of attending unnaturally to the unseen—we do that constant-ly—but of attending unnaturally to the *good* that is unseen.

Another problem with prayer is that God never says anything. What kind of conversation, what kind of personal relationship, can exist between two when one refuses to speak? Just once, why could God not say to me, audibly, two little words: "I'm listening"? Does not God's silence suggest rather that he is not listening and that my prayers amount to a whistling in the dark or, at best, mere self-therapy? Why not therefore avoid the frustration by attending to doctrine and relationships with other persons? And so I shout one last time at the towering stone cliff face, "God, why don't *you* ever speak?" And the echo of my own words is all I hear.

And yet . . .

Is the echo my voice or his? Why do I require that he speak in a voice that is recognizably not my own? Is it not more deeply satisfying to recognize—perhaps even in my own words—truths that are his? He could not act any more personally than by working in my very thoughts as I struggle to articulate words addressed to him. And so here, as on so many occasions, the echo of my prayer is his answer. The fact that I can talk to God as a child to a father is not a right but a privilege, explained first by Jesus and provided for us at terrible cost to him. Could a God who first goes to such lengths to tell me that he wants me to talk to him then not listen? He is present as often as the other invisible, silent objects of desire that occupy my mind. The privilege of address extends to every moment, however undignified, however brief, however tainted by my unworthiness. It is only my own refusal to pray and listen that prevents every moment of life from being lived in conscious contact with God.

Another objection we may have to prayer is that we do not get what we ask for. It does not help to argue that we should only praise God and not ask him for things, because most New Testament prayers involve requests. It does not help to argue that we should limit requests to "good things," because we either are not sure what is good ("this job or that?") and find vagueness dishonest ("I want her to marry me, but I'll just ask for your will to be done") or we are sure about what is good ("May Ed learn to love you") and it does not happen. In the few remaining cases where we do get what we want, it seems that the same result would have occurred whether or not anyone had prayed. After all, God has a universe to run, and he cannot disrupt the general plan of things by granting, even occasionally, the short-sighted petitions of various self-important dust specks.

And yet . . .

If God can indeed run the universe, he must be capable of more than a general plan of things. Even what I call the general plan—universe, human history, salvation—is unfathomably complex. Cannot the complexity of an infinite God extend to the interplay, the coordination of every seemingly unimportant human life, the hearing of every seemingly random desire, the granting of many seemingly selfish prayers? If this is true, I turn out to be very important, not a dust speck. Is it mere wish-fulfillment to imagine myself and my concerns to be of such specific importance to God? Not according to God, in the most clear message he ever sent to man: he suffered. The Son of God would not die for a dust speck, or even a million dust specks (which make only a cloud of dust). If, then, his love extends to each life and to the complexity of the actions and desires of each life, I do well to consider a deeper reason for ungranted desires than unheard prayer.

I wonder whether at the bottom of all our objections to prayer is not a simple disbelief in God. What a silly waste of time prayer is if he is not there, unless there might be some therapeutic value in certain forms of meditation common to most faiths. So we ask for things, and we try to hear things, all in an effort to discover if he is there. And then people like me invent subtle arguments to account for all the reasonable objections to his being there. If he is there, he is not going to compel anyone to believe by doing tricks when summoned. That is magic. And if he isn't there, the strange affection and confidence placed in him, that colossal Mistake, will continue to mystify the skeptic. On and on through the centuries we move, with just enough room for doubt, just enough room for faith, from the simplest minds to the greatest. This perpetual tension, this perpetual choice: Is this too an accident of evolution, or is it another aspect of the awesome complexity of God's plan? I can only continue on the premise that God wants us to live with that question, giving him the benefit of our doubt, continuing the conversation with him.

But even once we grant that it is good to talk to God, numerous questions come to mind about method. "How often should I pray?" "How should I address God?" "Am I allowed to ask to be healed of a head cold?" These questions fit categories of context, format, and content respectively, and they will serve as the scheme for the following description of the New Testament pattern. Numerous traditions about prayer, some helpful and some dangerous, have arisen in two thousand years. There is a tendency—perhaps stronger in this area than elsewhere—to use the New Testament merely to justify current practice. The challenge is to dig beneath the accumulated tradition of centuries to discover anew what prayer was to the first Christians and to consider what it can be to us.

CONTEXT

There is no specific instruction in the New Testament about the frequency of prayer. In Romans 12:12 Paul commands believers to be "constant in prayer" (RSV; cf. Col 4:2), but this cannot mean "nonstop"; in Acts 1:14 and 2:42 the same word is used to describe the devotion to prayer of the first converts, and there it is clear that prayer was *characteristic* of their activity but not *continuous*. Similarly, Paul admonishes believers to "pray without ceasing" (1 Thess 5:17 KJV), but it is evident from his use of the word elsewhere that he means by "unceasing" something stronger than "do this often" but weaker than "do nothing else" (Rom 1:9; 9:2; 1 Thess 1:3; 2:13).

Paul's recurrent references to his *prayers*(e.g., Rom 1:10; Eph 1:16; 1 Thess 1:2) imply specific times set aside for prayer. Even Jesus followed a pattern of specific times set aside for personal communion with the Father (e.g., Matt 14:23; Mark 14:32–39; Luke 5:16). But these patterns are not set forth as models, nor is there any reason given in Scripture for designating certain periods of time for prayer. Certainly access to God is unlimited, and he is always ready to hear a cry of praise or need uttered in the midst of some activity that demands most of our attention. But common sense dictates that scheduled blocks of time and regularity will allow for better communication than reliance on natural impulse. Certainly any friendship that merits the name will work that way. What a shame for a meaningful relationship with God to fall victim to the spiritual equivalent of the phrase, "Let's have lunch sometime."

Frequency of times of prayer is not an issue in the New Testament. There is no observable (much less required) pattern of daily prayer. On the other hand, there is no reason not to pray several times per day. Devout Jews in the first century set aside several periods in each day for prayer (in addition to prayer before meals; e.g., Matt 14:19; Acts 27:35; Rom 14:6). Paul may well have done this, but he did not command such a pattern. Old Testament texts speak equally of night time (Pss 63:6; 119:55) and early morning (Pss 5:3; 88:13) as good times of the day for prayer. But again, it is only tradition that has made a daily expectation of this pattern. Still, as in the case of designated periods for prayer, daily or more-than-daily frequency makes good sense. Given the busy schedules of most modern people, the expectation that a suitable period will simply appear is unrealistic; furthermore, daily routines are much more likely to adhere than weekly ones. Morning and evening are good times simply because we are usually better able to avoid interruption at those times.

Avoidance of interruption is the most obvious reason for the particular choice of a physical setting for prayer. The New Testament speaks of prayer in one's own room (Matt 6:6), on a mountain (Mark 6:46), in a deserted place (Luke 5:16), and on a housetop (Acts 10:9). Although there are no biblical texts to cite for support, it could certainly be argued that aids to concentration extend even to posture. Different people, or the same people at different times, pray best walking, sitting upright, kneeling, or even lying face down. Need it be added that such a list should not include being half-asleep, curled up under one's blanket?

PATTERN

To whom is my prayer addressed, and does it matter that I name him? In the New Testament, God is addressed normally as "Father" (Matt 6:9; Rom 8:15; 1 Peter 1:17). There is not a single instance of the Holy Spirit being addressed, and only a very few New Testament prayers are clearly addressed to Jesus. In John 14:14 Jesus promises that he will grant requests made of him. Paul refers to asking "the Lord" (his usual title for Jesus) for deliverance (2 Cor 12:8) and also to thanking him for strength (1 Tim 1:12).[1] The

___

[1]Other possible references are ambiguous: e.g., Acts 8:22, where it is not clear whether "the Lord" means God or Christ; and Eph 5:19 and Phil 4:10, where it is not clear that prayer is meant. The prayer "Maranatha" (1 Cor 16:22), translated "Come, O Lord!" (cf. Rev 22:20) may be understood as an expression of desire ("May our Lord come"), not a

overwhelming majority of references make God, not the Son or the Spirit, the one addressed in prayer. Why is this, if the few exceptions to the pattern demonstrate the *possibility* of addressing the Son, and if belief in a three-person coequal Godhead requires an understanding that Son and Spirit *hear* human prayer? The answer has to do with the problem of idolatry. Pagan prayer in the ancient world involved not only proper address to the deity but also choice of the correct deity to answer a given request. Statues or other images of the deities honored them and so were part of the proper procedure to induce them to perform. Such practices were scorned both by Jews and by Christians. The problem with idolatry was not that the true God hated art or respectful address but that he did not care to have his creatures try to turn him into a puppet.

In paganism, the god is reduced to manageable proportions. Similarly, in ancient and modern occult practice, the supernatural is supposedly brought under control by the power of the human mind. This is precisely where the danger occurs in prayer. We want to control God, and we are led to believe that our own will power (which we prefer to call "faith") and our own magic spells (which go by many names, including "specificity," "imaging," "persistence," etc.) will

---

prayer. Stephen's exclamation "Lord Jesus, receive my spirit" (Acts 7:59) occurs during a direct vision of the Lord. Even the passages mentioned in the text above are not indisputable. The audible response by Christ to Paul's prayer (2 Cor 12:9) may have influenced retroactively his reference to the Lord in 12:8. The authorship of 1 Timothy is disputed by some, and although I regard it as Pauline, I hesitate to base an argument about Paul's practice on a reference in a book of disputed authorship. But even if the authorship were undisputed, the reference must be acknowledged as very unusual. Furthermore, it may be that Paul, by virtue of his apostolic status, had direct access to Christ, which was not available to others. The John 14:14 passage was altered in many ancient manuscripts to omit reference to Christ as the one addressed in prayer. This does not necessarily shed doubt on the authenticity of the reference, but it is significant in that it reveals the early church's recognition of the oddity of such a reference.

accomplish that control. There is a tendency to divide up "duties" and to address the Father when we wish to praise the grand Creator and Judge, to address the Spirit when we want gifts or a sense of the divine presence, and to address Jesus when we want forgiveness, help, or understanding. One learns to choose the right name, depending on the subject matter of the prayer. Then, since the Son is the easiest to visualize, we imagine the gentle, companionable face from some painting or movie and talk to it. Some are even taught to picture this imagined figure talking to them, healing them, or doing other duties for them. All this is motivated, to be sure, by a desire to increase faith, to involve a person more personally with God in prayer. But such a deviation from the New Testament pattern and toward the pagan or occult pattern is dangerous. It runs the risk of reducing the Trinity to a three-choice vending machine and Jesus to an imaginary buddy.

The sequence of subject matter can become an exercise in superstition. Teachers of prayer technique commonly advise that praise should come first, follwed by confession, then prayer for others, and finally prayer for oneself. It is hardly coincidental that ancient pagan prayers followed much the same sequence. The idea in paganism was that one should make the god happy first so that he would be better disposed to grant one's request. Do we really expect the God of the universe to be flattered into submission to our desires by such an amateurish gimmick? Indeed, it may be better to avoid such a pattern by deliberately alternating kinds of prayer at different times. There can be no question of manufacturing sentiment or disguising true desires from a God who knows everything, so we may as well tell him what we think. What better context to begin practicing honesty than the context of prayer?

The Lord's Prayer (Matt 6:9–13; Luke 11:2–4) was given not as a pattern of sequence or subject matter but as a contrast to the wordiness and repetition of pagan prayers. Again, the danger is to attempt to manipulate God. Lengthy combinations of pious clichés acquired over time may give one a positive sense of one's own earnestness, but are not such productions the greatest barrier to sincerity? What friend or spouse would find such lengthy, articulate speeches believable as expressions of love, repentance, or need? Thus Jesus counsels that we should be brief and to the point about each item of prayer (Matt 6:7–13). Persistent repetition of the same request is approved in Luke 11:5–13 (cf. 18:1–8), and of course Jesus himself repeated his prayer in the Garden of Gethsemane (Mark 14:32–42). This pattern does not conflict with the prohibition of wordiness if the motive is not manipulation. The pagan repeats the spell or prayer, thinking that some benefit will result merely from the repeated pronunciation of the words. How ironic that the Lord's Prayer has been recited endlessly in this manner. By contrast, the believer who is persistent in prayer is merely expressing honestly, "This is still on my mind!"

At the end of many New Testament prayers comes the word "Amen." Today this is usually preceded by the phrase "in Jesus' name." Why use such a formula, except, practically speaking, to notify another person listening that the prayer is over?

"Amen" is the transliteration of an Aramaic expression often translated "truly" or "verily" at the beginning of many of the sayings of Jesus. The expression has to do with the certainty of a statement. As the final word of a prayer, it expresses a summary desire that everything in the preceding prayer may certainly happen (e.g., 1 Cor 16:24; Gal 6:18). Thus the word itself is a prayer: "Please, God, do all of this."

To add "in Jesus' name" is redundant but certainly not harmful. No New Testament prayer ends with the formula, but prayer is commanded to be addressed to the Father in the name of Jesus (John 15:16; Eph 5:20). Baptism (Acts 2:38;

10:48), healing (Acts 3:6; James 5:14), and justification (1 Cor 6:11) are all accomplished "in the name of Jesus Christ." The meaning of the phrase is revealed most clearly in the question asked of the apostles in Acts 4:7: "By what power or what name did you do this [healing]?" Identification of oneself with the "name" of another meant appropriating the qualities, including the power, of that individual. As an element of prayer, identification of the name of Jesus is a more specific way of saying "Amen": "Please, God, in that I am identified with Jesus and thus with your power, do all of this."

CONTENT

A survey of the subject matter of New Testament prayers yields results that seem inconsistent with modern practice. The most common subject of prayer is thanksgiving for the faith and love of others (e.g., Col 1:3–4; 1 Thess 1:2–3; Philem 1:4–5). The large number of references may be due to the fact that Paul likes to begin his letters positively by communicating the content of his prayers of gratitude. But this fact does not lessen the importance of the subject; encouragement of the faith and love of believers receives far more attention than any other subject in the New Testament, and it is natural to expect a great deal of thanksgiving for the community God is building. Indeed, if we add to this category requests for an increase in the faith and love and particularly the wisdom of others (e.g., John 17:11; Phil 1:9; Col 4:12), "concern for other believers" is far and away the most common subject matter of New Testament prayers, with nearly forty references to it.

Two other common subjects of prayer are thanksgiving for the benefits of salvation (e.g., Rom 7:25; 1 Cor 15:57; Col 1:12) and personal requests for deliverance from harm or evil. The requests for deliverance are not merely expressions of the self-preservation instinct but desires that the recipients' safety will allow further preaching (e.g., Rom 15:31–32; Phil 1:19–26; 2 Thess 3:1–2).

After these categories, comprising about ten references each, it is inappropriate to speak of categories, because the numbers of references are so small. What is more interesting is to note that other subjects of prayer mentioned in the New Testament, and perhaps dominant today, were apparently *not* major concerns in the New Testament era. Among these less dominant subjects are prayer for enemies (Matt 5:44; Mark 11:25; Luke 23:34; Acts 7:60), physical health (Acts 28:8; 2 Cor 12:8; James 5:13–16; 3 John 1:2), confession of sin (Luke 18:13; James 5:16; 1John 1:9), personal guidance (Acts 1:24; possibly James 1:5), and spiritual gifts (1 Cor 12:31; 14:13).

The comparative lack of attention given to these concerns hardly means that they are illegitimate items for prayer, but it does reveal the New Testament stress on corporate rather than individual concerns. It may be that the seeming lack of interest in personal desires arises in part from the public nature of the documents or from the fact that neither direction nor example were needed to encourage requests for personal guidance or gifts. Furthermore, the Psalms may supply sufficient warrant for the expression of personal concerns. Nevertheless, it is worth considering whether modern thought about prayer may have turned us too far inward. The danger is that our prayer life may reflect the inadequacy of our response to God and to others: it may be fundamentally self-centered, even narcissistic.

If this caution is legitimate, it may shed some light on a difficult group of passages that tell the believer simply, "Whatever you ask in prayer, you will receive, if you have faith" (Matt 21:22 RSV; Mark 11:24). This promise normally includes some qualification even beyond faith. The petition must be for something good (Matt 7:11), it must involve agreement between believers (Matt 18:19), it must be requested in Jesus' name (John 14:13–14; 15:16; 16:23–24), it must agree with God's will (1 John 5:14–16), and it must be grounded in obedience (John 15:7, 10; 1 John 3:22). The composite picture that emerges complements the picture just seen of New Testament subjects of prayer. Prayer about subjects dominant in the New Testament is most likely to fit the intent of the statement "Ask anything."

The promise, then, is not a blank check. It is more like a gift certificate for a particular store. And without extending the analogy too far, it is useful to add that the store can be entered only from a certain narrow road.

Does this mean that obedient people get their requests granted because they are obedient or because they are more likely to ask for the right things? As a disobedient person, I can only guess. Perhaps obedient people differ not in that they *get* more but in that they are more apt to *see* what they get. I only know that when I am most aware of God's presence, I begin to become grateful *in detail*.

Only prayer, which *is* obedience in one sense, allows for the recognition of answered prayer, which *is* obedience in another sense. The ascending, spiraling strands of request, gratitude, and obedience ultimately merge at a point perhaps beyond our experience but not beyond our comprehension.

MEDITATION

The subject of answers to prayers brings up the question of the role of listening in prayer. Conspicuously absent from the New Testament material is reference to meditation, and only rarely is there evidence of reception of audible—or inaudible—messages from God (2 Cor 12:9; possibly also Acts 23:11). Where messages are given, the phenomenon is clearly abnormal.

What then of Old Testament passages like Psalm 63:6 (RSV): "I meditate on thee in the watches of the night"? It is crucial to understand that this and other Old Testament references to meditation are not passive but active. They involve no emptying of the mind (even as a preliminary to worship) but rather the filling of the mind. Without exception, the object of meditation named is God's being (Ps 63:6), his works (Pss 77:12; 119:27), or, most often, his commands as revealed in Scripture (Pss 1:2; 119:48, 78, 99). There is no question here of special messages, which are the domain of prophecy, or of mystical union, which is the domain of Eastern religion. Modern meditation techniques that encourage mind-emptying as a prelude to worship, imagining as an expression of faith in making requests, and listening for voices as a means of seeking guidance have no basis in biblical practice. Their emphasis on the creative power of the individual mind leads easily to self-delusion.

ECSTATIC LANGUAGE

Whether it falls under "content" or "format," ecstatic language or "speaking in tongues" must be considered in a discussion of prayer. The phenomenon of nonlanguage vocal articulation is not unique to Christian experience. Psychological researchers have documented ecstatic speech on the part of spirit mediums and schizophrenics, and the phenomenon is reported in religious sects of other cultures, especially among animists.[2] This should cause no more disturbance to the believer or the tongues-speaker than the fact that members of these religious groups also practice preaching or teaching— or love. What it does suggest is that ecstatic speech is a human phenomenon that is uniquely Christian or a gift only to the extent that it is used to God's glory. Paul gives specific instructions for its use by Christians in 1 Corinthians 14:1–

---

[2]See H. N. Maloney and A. A. Lovekin, *Glossolalia* (New York: Oxford University Press, 1985).

40. These include subservience to "higher" gifts such as prophecy (14:1, 19, 39), regulation of number and sequence of speakers (14:26–27), and accompaniment by interpretation (14:5–28). Paul may have needed to give these directives because the earlier, spontaneous group response to the initial gift of salvation (cf. Acts 2:4; 10:46; 19:6) had become institutionalized as a supposed "proof" of the Corinthians' power and of their love for God.

Naturally, then as now, this mistaken view leads to the imposition of subtle pressure on those who do not participate in the experience and often creates division within the group. Paul argues that the experience is essentially personal rather than public (14:18–19; cf. Rom 8:26) and that it is not available to all (12:30; cf. 12:1–29), even though it would be good for all to speak in tongues (14:5). His overriding thesis is consistent with my earlier observations about the appropriate content of prayer: ecstatic speech, if it is to increase the faith and love of an individual or group, must be accompanied by a rational interpretation that gives specific information or direction. In a word, it must be *upbuilding* (14:5, 12–13, 26).

· 4 ·

Dependence:
"Leave Behind All Your Possessions"

Jesus is the central figure in the Bible, not only in that his death accomplished our forgiveness but also in that his life gave us a pattern to follow. Indeed, one of his followers later wrote that "whoever claims to live in him must walk as Jesus did" (1 John 2:6). This idea of the centrality of Jesus is obvious when we consider his teaching about humility, prayer, and forgiveness—subjects about which he spoke plainly and frequently. But it is curious that with respect to the most frequent of all subjects in his teaching, the use of wealth, he is often made peripheral rather than central. The tendency is not to walk after him but to walk around him. Even those who make the strongest claim to taking the Bible literally resist taking Jesus literally in this area. To be sure, there are other, less demanding models of behavior in the economic sphere in other parts of the Bible. Are the harsh demands of Jesus only a curiosity?

Many readers will find this chapter very disturbing and perhaps contrary to the traditional teaching of most Christian churches. There is a double irony in this for me as a writer. For one thing, I cannot be accused of interpreting Scripture to justify myself, because I must admit at the outset that I am far from obedience to the teaching I will describe. On the other hand, considerable study over a long period of time enables me to write with some authority.[1] So while others might demean their knowledge but offer self-justifying recommendations, I can only claim to understand all too well a standard of which I fall short.

It may appear strange that an explanation of New Testament teaching about wealth should find itself in a part of the book concerned with the individual's relation to God rather than one of the following parts. We usually read Jesus' radical teachings as an impetus to give our tithes to the church or to practice social justice in the world. But the essence of his teaching is more personal. Our conduct with our possessions reveals the condition of our hearts. Dependence on God is not only an attitude, then, but also an activity. And according to Jesus, there is perhaps no activity more revealing of one's relation to God than one's use of money.

It is important to begin by rejecting in the strongest possible terms the notion that the harsh demands of Jesus were meant only for the time of the disciples or only to make people aware of how much they need forgiveness. The Gospels were written thirty to forty years after Jesus' public ministry to inform and instruct believers about what Jesus did and how they were expected to live. These believers clearly understood that the teaching was meant for them. If Jesus' teachings were relevant forty years later, why not two thousand years later? Jesus himself made it very clear that only those who obey his teaching will one day be welcomed into the kingdom (Matt 7:21–27). Later in the chapter we will consider possible exceptions or alterations of Jesus'

---

[1]Thomas E. Schmidt, *Hostility to Wealth in the Synoptic Gospels* (Sheffield, England, 1987). This book is the published version of my Ph.D. dissertation at Cambridge University. The biblical passages treated in this chapter are considered there in much greater depth.

teaching within the Gospels, but at least for now we must consider the material at face value. We must beware of the tendency to interpret the words of Jesus in a way that justifies our own way of living. We may accept or dismiss the teaching only after we have considered it honestly.

THE COMMAND TO SELL ALL

As a familiar story repeated in three of the Gospels (Matt 19:16–30; Mark 10:17–31; Luke 18:18–30), the account of the rich young ruler is a good place to begin. Jesus responded to the man's question about eternal life by telling him to sell all his possessions, give to the poor, and follow Jesus. The man refused. Jesus went on to explain how difficult it is for rich people to get into heaven. If one wonders whether Jesus meant "very difficult" or "impossible," one need only attempt to insert a camel through the eye of a needle.[2] The disciples reacted in amazement to such a rigorous demand, and Jesus responded that it is indeed impossible without God. This is hardly a statement that the rich man will be saved anyway because God will forgive him. Such an explanation would make Jesus' teaching up to that point meaningless. It is obvious that the disciples got the point, because they responded with a question about the adequacy of their own "leaving all": "We have left everything to follow you! What then will there be for us?" (Matt 19:27). Jesus affirmed this response and added that everyone who acts the same way will get the same reward. He did not digress into a discussion of God's grace in spite of man's disobedience: he spoke of man's action, which must appropriate God's power.

Another important passage is Luke 14:25–33, which

---

[2]Attempts to shrink the camel (by the claim that Jesus meant "cable" rather than "camel") or to enlarge the needle (by the medieval legend that there was a small gate in the wall of ancient Jerusalem called "the needle's eye") are creative, but desperate.

ends with the disturbing statement, "So therefore, no one of you can be My disciple who does not give up all his own possessions" (NASB). Two parables precede this command— one about a tower-builder and the other about a king going to war. These parables are usually described as encouragements to "count the cost" of discipleship before deciding to follow Jesus, but such an interpretation makes a very rough connection with the suggested application of verse 33. How does renunciation of possessions follow from calculation? The parables should be understood as a warning: the person who plans a task with inadequate resources is foolish. The implication is that one's own earthly securities will not earn eternal reward; therefore, they must be abandoned. Efforts to spiritualize verse 33 fail. Jesus is not commanding followers to give up a nebulous "everything": the word used here for possessions is used elsewhere in the New Testament only for material goods (e.g., Matt 19:21; Luke 12:33). Nor does he say that one must be merely "willing" to give up all: the verb used here is used elsewhere in the New Testament only for actual abandonment (e.g., Mark 6:46; Acts 18:18).

There is a tendency to rationalize the possession of wealth by claiming, "In my heart I have given it all to God." This may follow from the justifiable position that one's attitudes and motives matter as much to God as one's actions, or it may be a thinly disguised desire to eat one's cake and have it too. Jesus, in contrasting God and wealth, did not allow this option. One or the other, God or wealth, is one's *employer* (Matt 6:24; Luke 16:13), and the one that is not served is hated. Attempts to define "hate" as "love less" fly in the face of universal biblical usage. In this context, it is best to understand the practical application of "hatred" as "abandonment," as in Luke 14:26, where Jesus tells disciples to hate their families. It is ironic that Jesus' words "For where your treasure is, there your heart will be also" (Matt 6:21) are often used to justify the possession of wealth. This is done by reversing the order of the propositions to read "Where your heart is, there will your treasure be also." Jesus says the opposite: what one does with money, according to this verse, *reveals* the state of the heart.

There are numerous other troubling passages. Jesus concluded the parable of the rich fool in Luke 12:21 with the warning that people must be rich toward God rather than lay up treasure for themselves. Later in the same chapter he commanded his disciples to apply this by selling possessions and giving to the poor. Luke 16:9 commands believers, "Use worldly wealth to gain friends for yourselves, so that when it is gone, you will be welcomed into eternal dwellings." The command could be paraphrased "Give away possessions so that when you die God will give you eternal reward." In the story of the rich man and Lazarus (Luke 16:19–31 RSV), the rich man is guilty not only for neglecting the poor man at his gate but also for being "dressed in purple and fine linen" and for "feasting sumptuously every day." When Jesus explained the parable of the sower (Mark 4:14–20), he described people whose initial response to the truth is destroyed by "the cares of this world, and the deceitfulness of riches, and the lusts of other things" (KJV). The second phrase is particularly strong because it describes wealth as *deceitful*. Is this too harsh? Jesus is even more harsh on at least one other occasion. When the money-loving Pharisees scoffed at Jesus' teaching about choosing between God and wealth (Luke 16:10–14), Jesus responded, "What is highly valued among men is detestable in God's sight." Jesus is not attacking pride here—no one exalts pride—but the *cause* of pride: the possession of wealth. The word "detestable" could not be stronger—it is used elsewhere in reference to idolatry, the worst sin imaginable (e.g., Ezra 9:11; Rom 2:22).

EXCEPTIONS IN THE GOSPELS?

The composite effect of these passages can be devastating to those who have not been trained to respond in a way that lessens their impact. There are several ways to attempt such a "softening." One is to point to examples of rich believers in the Gospels who are not condemned. Zacchaeus (Luke 19:1–10) is the example most often cited. Jesus announced the salvation of this man after he pledged, "I give half of my possessions to the poor, and if I have cheated anybody out of anything, I will pay back four times the amount." It is a mistake to read this as a justification for retaining half of one's wealth (but how many go even as far as that?). Zacchaeus retained half his wealth, not to sustain a comfortable lifestyle but to channel his giving to the appropriate sources. His former victims would hardly be impressed by the news that he had given their money to the poor instead of to themselves. And to make fourfold restitution to those he had defrauded would quickly deplete the remaining half of his estate. Zacchaeus, then, is not an example of the acceptably wealthy but a contrast to the rich young man in the previous chapter who would not give away his possessions.

Joseph of Arimathea (Matt 27:57), the man who provided for the burial of Jesus, is described as rich only in Matthew's gospel. This may well be an allusion to Isaiah 53:9, which says that "he was assigned a grave with the wicked and with the rich in his death." Rather than being an encouragement for rich believers, then, the text may be one more indirect condemnation of wealth. But even if Joseph of Arimathea or some other example is found, it is hardly reasonable to use an occasional narrative reference to overturn numerous clear and lengthy teaching passages addressed directly to disciples.

In Luke 22:35–36 Jesus tells his disciples that, in contrast to his earlier instruction, they should now carry purses, bags, and swords. Is this one story intended to invalidate the previous teaching of Jesus about wealth (and nonviolence), to usher in a new period of less demanding discipleship? This can hardly be the case. The passage occurs in only one Gospel and in a place where the point to be made is Jesus' association with rebels at the time of his arrest, not his expectations for ongoing behavior. It is not sensible to take such an incident out of context in order to soften the impact of a larger body of teaching. The subject comprises nearly one-fourth of the teaching of Jesus as recorded in Matthew, Mark, and Luke, and it is impossible to escape the conclusion that those three gospel writers included so much without intending it to have some relevance to their readers.

The disturbing truth is that Matthew, Mark, and Luke present a consistently negative picture of wealth. There simply are no significant exceptions, and whatever straws one attempts to grasp crumble when one considers the repeated and clear statements directed by Jesus to people who want to follow him. The possession of wealth creates a false sense of security, the opposite of that dependence on God without which no one will be saved. The texts do not give a precise definition of wealth other than to call into question anything that provides security beyond a day (Matt 6:19–20; Mark 12:44). But even with a less radical definition of wealth, almost every reader will feel the sting. The more desperately one looks for exceptions to the teaching, the less likely anything he finds can qualify as an exception.

THE PRACTICE OF THE EARLY CHURCH

Is generosity and dependence on God taken to such a radical and literal extreme anywhere but in the Gospels? Could it be that the church recognized that Jesus' demands on the subject were meant only for the period of his earthly career, even though all of his other ethical teaching was meant for ongoing application?

A quick or selective survey of material elsewhere in the New Testament might lead to this conclusion. Paul commands generosity (2 Cor 8:1–9:15; Gal 6:6–10; 1 Tim 6:17–19; cf. 1 John 3:17–18), but he does not mention giving *all*. Instead, his emphasis seems to be on contentment with one's present circumstances (Phil 4:11–12; 1 Tim 6:6–10; cf. Heb 13:5–7), and he does not warn against the retention of possessions. The early church in Acts practiced community of goods (2:44–46; 4:32–37), but the emphasis here is on unity and the meeting of needs, not dispossession to the point of dependence. There is no record of the subsequent history of this communal economy. It may have failed to attract or retain members and quickly became a group within the group.

If these were the only passages outside the Gospels on the subject of wealth, we might be able to construct an argument that, for some unknown reason, after Jesus departed the situation changed to an acceptance of wealth as long as it is accompanied by a measure of generosity. But there are several passages that destroy this notion. James 2:1–10 and 5:1–6 contain strong condemnations of the rich and use much of the same vocabulary that Jesus used in the Gospels. Revelation 3:17–18 (cf. 18:16–20) and 1 Corinthians 4:8 (cf. 2 Cor 6:10) also put wealth in a negative light, equating its possession with pride.

There are two additional passages in 1 Corinthians that may shed light on the attitude of the primitive church. In 1 Corinthians 13:3, Paul maintains, "If I give all I possess to the poor and surrender my body to the flames, but have not love, I gain nothing." This statement reveals two important facts. One is that Paul was aware of radical dispossession and considered it a commendable option, provided that it be accompanied by love. The other activities that he lists in the context (speaking in tongues, prophesying, possessing knowledge, and suffering martyrdom) are all good; and this last pairing, of the dispossession of goods with something as significant as martyrdom, implies that dispossession is highly admirable behavior. The second fact suggested by this statement is that dispossession was, by the time Paul wrote 1 Corinthians (c. 55 A.D.), a rare practice. Martyrdom, the activity with which it is paired here, was not common in the church until some time later. The impression is that here are two examples of complete but unusual obedience.

We may get more insight into the practice of the church at this time from an earlier passage in 1 Corinthians. Paul recommends celibacy in chapter 7 because he does not want believers to be weighed down by worldly concerns. In 7:30–31, as part of his concluding remarks on this theme, he urges "those who buy [to act] as though they had no goods, and those who deal with the world as though they had no dealings with it. For the form of this world is passing away" (RSV). Paul makes these remarks in passing without addressing the questions that we are asking about possessions, but it is not hard to imagine how his principle might apply if he were to turn his attention from marriage to economics. He would maintain that living without wealth is best, because the one without possessions is not apt to be anxious about preserving them. That person's concern will be for the kingdom, for dependence on God. This is essentially the same teaching as that found in the Gospels. Far from overturning the radical demand of the teaching of Jesus, Paul affirms it in principle— and probably in his own practice.

IS POVERTY THE ANSWER?

A Jewish rabbi, writing a commentary on the Gospels, argued that the teaching of Jesus on this subject is impractical, even foolhardy. If many people took it seriously, the result would be dependence on other people, even though this might occur in the name of dependence on God. True poverty is not a state of blessedness but a state of misery, constricting the soul and leading to further misery through political turmoil. No one who has seen the back streets of Cairo or Delhi can idealize poverty. The world does not need more poor people. Instead, some contend, we need wealthy people who manage resources wisely to provide necessities and opportunities for those who need help. Good management, not voluntary poverty, is the appropriate behavior for responsible people. We will only add to the social problems created by poverty if we add ourselves to the number of poor people.

This perspective is persuasive in many respects. It could be added that voluntary poverty is a contradiction in terms, since real poverty is a miserable state largely because it is hopeless, whereas the corporate executive who gives up "all" to move to the ghetto could probably go back to the corporate life at some point. And even such a person who remains poor has the consolations of having made the choice and of expecting a reward in the afterlife for such dramatic obedience. The truly poor person lacks such consolations.

It is interesting to speculate about how Jesus might respond to our modern arguments. It seems to me doubtful that he would say, "I didn't mean for you to take my words at face value," or, "I guess I hadn't really thought of the social and economic implications of all this." I think his response would be more along these lines: "You will indeed create a social problem if you all obey me. But look at the problems you have created by not obeying me. Lazarus is dying at your feet, and the whole world looks on your Christian nation as the great waster of things necessary, the great glutton for things unneccessary. You call yourself a "steward" because you take a minute each month to send me a check from your excess. You observe that others who call me Lord do not do more. Which of those others is your Lord? Will you refuse to take the first step behind me because you fear some later step? Will you keep your Mercedes because you are worried about losing your toothbrush?"

STRIVING FOR OBEDIENCE

The teaching of the New Testament on the subject of wealth, because it is so hard-hitting, is perhaps the best example of the ethic of striving described in the introductory chapter. To spiritualize the teaching, to look for exceptions, to limit the application to a particular time or group, to focus on the impractability of obedience—these are weak efforts at self-justification that fail to do justice to the clear intent of the texts. To the extent that we are not obedient to that radical demand, we are not yet obedient. There is no plateau along the way that one can point to and say, "This is giving enough" or "That is an appropriately simple lifestyle." And yet to face this challenge and to refuse in horror even to move toward obedience is to follow in the steps of the rich young ruler. Somewhere between refusing and arriving is the indefinable but essential activity of *trying*. It may involve small, halting, steps away from luxury and toward simplicity. It must involve continual, serious self-evaluation. It will probably require cries for mercy in the midst of failure. And most certainly, it will require appropriation of the power of God for the movement toward *his* standard of success.

Part II

The Believer in Relation to Other Believers

Therefore, as we have opportunity, let us do good to all people, especially to those who belong to the family of believers.

Galatians 6:10

Now that you have purified yourselves by obeying the truth so that you have sincere love for your brothers, love one another deeply, from the heart.

1 Peter 1:22

• 5 •

Sympathy:

"Bear One Another's Burdens"

I have not known a great amount of pain or sorrow. My small experience, however, illustrates a truth that the reader may expand to meet a greater need.

The darkest time in my life was a period of anguish and confusion following a broken romantic relationship. For over a year, I struggled to overcome feelings of betrayal and guilt, and I poured out my thoughts to many caring individuals. Most gave irrelevant advice based on their own experiences. Some offered helpful spiritual insights, but these insights I already understood. Others expressed pity or anger, which fed my worst tendencies toward self-justification and resentment. But one woman—oddly enough, one who did not know me well—gave something entirely different. She listened very carefully as I told my story. And then, in the midst of the description of my hurt, she began to cry. She had no advice, no insight, no anger—she merely wept. And for the first time in that long process I knew what it was to receive *sympathy*. The word, like its Latin synonym, "compassion," means literally, "to suffer with." My friend at that moment gave nothing more, and nothing less, than the sharing of my pain.

There was another One long ago who gave the same. John 11 tells the story of Jesus' visit to the house of Martha and Mary, who were mourning over the death of their brother Lazarus. The story follows Jesus, on the way to the scene of grief, aware ahead of time that he would raise Lazarus from the dead (vv. 4, 15, 23). As a symbol of Jesus' power over eternal life (vv. 23–26), this raising of Lazarus is of course the main point of the narrative. Thus it is all the more surprising that the following scene occurs in the middle of the chapter:

> When Jesus saw [Mary] weeping, and the Jews who had come along with her also weeping, he was deeply moved in spirit and troubled. "Where have you laid him?" he asked. "Come and see, Lord," they replied. Jesus wept. (John 11:33–35)

It is not surprising to see that Jesus felt compassion when confronted by human need (e.g., Matt 14:14; 15:32; Luke 7:13). What is remarkable in this story is the timing: Jesus responded to the grief of others just moments before he would transform their grief to wonder and joy. He did not weep for Lazarus; he wept for Mary and the other mourners. The compassion of God in Jesus is his choice, an expression of love. Having all the answers, having all the power, he still chose to hurt with those who hurt, simply because to do so is to love.

THE GOD OF ALL COMFORT

The majority of the New Testament material about compassion comes from what may be, to some, a surprising source: the apostle Paul. The caricature of Paul as an argumentative, patronizing, issue-oriented person is contradicted by the evidence. Certainly he was willing and able to dispute about theological matters, and, as we would expect from an accepted figure of authority, he usually writes in a directive manner. But the central issue for him is always the need of the people he loves. His letters often begin with an overflow of thanksgiving on their behalf and end with numerous personal greetings. He is careful always to acknowledge and praise co-workers, and he expresses an intense longing to see face-to-face those to whom he writes. When he leaves one group for the last time, there is great mourning (Acts 20:37–38), and when another group grieves to see him go, he cries, "Why are you weeping and breaking my heart?" (21:13) His was a great mind, to be sure, but it was accompanied by a great heart.

Paul's most explicit example of sympathy occurs in his correspondence with the Corinthians. In the letter that we know as 2 Corinthians, he wrote to a group of believers that came into being through his work but later disputed his authority, spurned his efforts toward reconciliation, and finally repented. Paul, having been rejected by them, had to wait for months in agony over them until he received the news of their repentence from his emissary, Titus. The letter of 2 Corinthians is his response to this good news. It is instructive to observe in detail the manner in which he begins this letter: it is perhaps the best example in the New Testament of someone practicing the behavior that he recommends elsewhere.

Remember that Paul finds these people down and squirming—they are ideally suited to be made victims of condescension, advice, and manipulative expressions of his own hurt. Instead, after the standard opening greeting, he performs a feat of empathy that is nothing short of incredible:

> Praise be to the God and Father of our Lord Jesus Christ, the Father of compassion and the God of all comfort, who comforts us in all our troubles, so that we can comfort those in any trouble with the comfort we ourselves have received from God. For just as the sufferings of Christ flow over into our lives, so also through Christ our

comfort overflows. If we are distressed, it is for your comfort and salvation; if we are comforted, it is for your comfort, which produces in you patient endurance of the same sufferings we suffer. And our hope for you is firm, because we know that just as you share in our sufferings, so also you share in our comfort. (2 Cor 1:3–7)

The obvious stress here is on the word *comfort* , which occurs ten times in five verses. When he picks up the theme again in chapter 7, Paul uses the word seven more times (elsewhere in his writings the word occurs only rarely). But there is much more to this paragraph than the concentration of vocabulary. Paul uses the term and constructs the paragraph in such a way that he draws the Corinthians' attention away from their shame, not by ignoring it, but by making it the prerequisite of growth. He begins by drawing their attention to God, not to himself. It is the character of "the Father of compassion and God of all comfort" to receive with open arms the one who is sorry (cf. Luke 15:20), and Paul immediately directs their repentance away from himself as the victim and toward God as the comforter. The brilliant twist from this point onward is that he likens their comfort in receiving God's forgiveness to his own comfort in receiving their repentance. By so doing he makes the painful process *shared* by them the means of God's comfort. By avoiding a discussion of the sequence or the cause of the suffering in view, Paul focuses on the essential idea: having shared this experience, they are all, Paul included, "being changed into his likeness from one degree of glory to another" (3:18 RSV).

Paul demonstrates what today we call *empathy* (literally, "entering into [someone else's] suffering") by relating his remarks to his own experience of suffering. Although he is an authority figure, although he is knowledgeable, these qualifications do not give him the right to address the Corinthians on this delicate subject. Paul has the right to speak of comfort only because he *understands*, and he has the ability to

understand only because *he has suffered*. He speaks of his own
suffering in strongly personal terms in the opening chapters
(1:8–10; 2:4; 2:12–13) and in more general terms later in the
letter (4:7–12; 6:8–10; 11:24–29). His own experience gives
him confidence that they will see their own redemption in the
process of repentance:

> Even if I caused you sorrow by my letter, I do not regret
> it. Though I did regret it—I see that my letter hurt you,
> but only for a little while—yet now I am happy, not
> because you were made sorry, but because your sorrow
> led you to repentance. For you became sorrowful as God
> intended and so were not harmed in any way by us.
> Godly sorrow brings repentance that leads to salvation
> and leaves no regret, but worldly sorrow brings death.
> See what this godly sorrow has produced in you: what
> earnestness, what eagerness to clear yourselves, what
> indignation, what alarm, what longing, what concern,
> what readiness to see justice done. At every point you
> have proved yourselves to be innocent in this matter. So
> even though I wrote to you, it was not on account of the
> one who did the wrong or of the injured party, but rather
> that before God you could see for yourselves how devoted
> to us you are. By all this we are encouraged. (2 Cor. 7:8–
> 13)

As a final noteworthy detail of this incident, we should
not overlook Paul's *elevation* of the Corinthians. This is what
distinguishes empathy or sympathy from pity: pity merely
drops a tear or two from on high. Paul, on the contrary,
expresses his own dependence on those whom he comforts.
His opening paragraph, for example, ends with these words:
"You also must help us by prayer, so that many will give
thanks on our behalf for the blessing granted us in answer to
many prayers" (1:11 RSV; cf. Phil 1:19; 1 Thess 3:7–8). Later
in the same chapter, he expresses his desire that they be
proud of him (v. 14) and that they see him not as one who
lords it over them but as one who works with them, for their

joy (v. 24). His term for them here, "co-workers," is one that he uses elsewhere exclusively for his own associate evangelists. Here is a man who is so freed from the burden of his own interests that he is able to carry with grace the burden of others—even when that burden is an offense against him. Indeed, the principle, like this example, is closely tied to forgiveness. The command to "bear one another's burdens" (Gal 6:2 RSV) follows this tenderly worded exhortation: "Brothers, if someone is caught in a sin, you who are spiritual should restore him gently. But watch yourself, or you also may be tempted" (Gal 6:1).

"BOWELS AND MERCIES"

Paul's example in 2 Corinthians reflects his recommendation in other contexts. In Romans 12:15 (RSV) he exhorts believers to "weep with those who weep," in 1 Thessalonains 4:18 he urges the bereaved to comfort one another, and in Philippians 2:1 he begins his request for unity with an appeal to his audience's "tenderness and compassion."

The pairing of these terms is instructive. Sympathy requires imagination and will, whereas affection is the more emotive facet of burden bearing. In the ancient world, the heart was associated not only with emotion but more generally with decision making. Deep emotion, especially grief, was associated with the physical response typical of it: sensation in the lower abdomen. Thus the Greek expression to indicate strong affection means literally for one's bowels to move. The King James Version therefore translates this phrase "bowels and mercies." The pairing occurs again in Philippians 2:1 and Colossians 3:12–13 (cf. 2 Corinthians 1:3, 1 Peter 3:8, and Ephesians 4:32). Ephesians 4:32 and Colossians 3:12–13, which use the terms interchangeably, are particularly valuable because they were written at about the same time and because in both instances the words are used to motivate the same behavior: forgiveness of others.

JESUS AS EXAMPLE

On numerous occasions in the Gospels we read that Jesus was "moved with compassion" (Matt 9:36; Mark 1:41; Luke 7:13), and the text invariably uses the term for abdominal sensation. A contemporary expression to convey the thought might be "his guts were wrenched." It is significant that in these passages, as in John 11 discussed above, Jesus is shown as deeply, *physically* responsive to human suffering. Compassion is a character trait of God in the Old Testament (e.g., Exod 22:27; Ps 51:1; Isa 54:7–8); but in the gut-wrenching of Jesus, God takes a costly step toward proving it. The final, decisive step is through the Garden ("My soul is overwhelmed with sorrow to the point of death," Matt 26:38) and to the Cross ("My God, my God, why have you forsaken me?" Mark 15:34). In that place love—the only love that could do it—went beyond sharing suffering to *taking* suffering. There, truly, burdens were borne. And so these triumphant words could be written: "For we do not have a high priest who is unable to *sympathize* with our weaknesses, but we have one who has been tempted in every way, just as we are—yet was without sin" (Heb 4:15, italics mine).

The suffering of Jesus was not a mistake. The humanity of Jesus is not a compromise. Our attention to his divinity sometimes allows us to miss the importance of his physical nature. God in Jesus demonstrates that infinite knowledge is not factual but intimate. The words "I can speak because I understand; I can understand because I have suffered" are written with his blood.

THE WAY OF BURDEN BEARING

Sympathy is, fundamentally, an exercise in imagination. At times, especially when the sufferer is a close friend or family member, it is natural to see the situation through another's eyes. At such times the identity of the other is so closely bound to one's own that the experience is easily shared. But more often, our natural inclination is to put as much spatial or emotional distance as we can between ourselves and pain. We avoid suffering, so we avoid sufferers. Or, if sufferers are unavoidable, we produce advice and spiritual platitudes.

Sympathy, however, is work. And of course, by definition, it is painful. Perhaps that is why it is described by New Testament writers not as a quality but rather as an activity. Sympathy is something rather like an uncomfortable but functional garment that one must *put on* (Col 3:12). Our natural desire is to do without it.

In practical terms, sympathy means concentrating on the meaning of another person's words, carefully probing where necessary for clarification. It requires silence when the impulse is to "trade stories." When a few words are appropriate, they should be chosen to reveal understanding rather than a "solution." In the enormous space thus emptied of these and other self-defense mechanisms there is now room for imagination. What, precisely, is this person experiencing? How does this person see the situation, the future, the past, God, others involved, even me? Have I known something similar? Because my experience was not exactly the same, I must avoid the creeping temptation to impose my own experience on this situation. I must let the *other* be the point of reference. If I cannot find a personal reference point, it might be most loving to communicate *that*. But if I can find a personal reference point, or if I can imagine what the sufferer knows and feels now, the crucial moment comes. Knowing that God wants it—indeed, He set the pattern for it—the next step is to seek to enter into that person's suffering. It will be easy to know when I have done it, because it will hurt. Then I have loved as God loves. I can forgive or comfort, and there too I participate in the character of God, by the power of God. Communication of care to the other at this point becomes natural because it is now *true*. A tear, a word, an embrace, and the love has flowed like water through the channels for which it was intended: God suffered, a person suffers, God's child suffers with that person. All three are physical, all three are true. And if the saying is sure that "all truth is God's truth," then all tears are God's tears. He makes them all, he receives them all, he counts them all. To bear a burden is to participate most intimately in the character of the God who is love.

• 6 •

Unity:
"Be of the Same Mind"

When unbelievers hear the words of God on our lips they marvel at their beauty and greatness. But afterwards, when they notice that our actions are unworthy of the words we speak, they turn from this to scoffing, and say that it is a myth and a delusion. When, for instance, they hear from us that God says, "It is no credit to you if you love those who love you, but it is to your credit if you love your enemies and those who hate you," when they hear these things, they are amazed at such overwhelming goodness. But when they see that we fail to love not only those who hate us, but even those who love us, then they laugh at us and scoff at the Name.

This sad commentary on Christian unity could have been written last week. The fact is that it was written around the turn of the century—the *first* century. It is an excerpt from a letter by the Roman bishop Clement to the believers living in Corinth.[1] A careful study of the period will disappoint those who think longingly of the early church as a time when

---

[1] 2Clement 13:2. Many scholars regard the letter as inauthentic. If this is true, it may have been written closer to the middle of the second century.

believers stood together as one in belief and practice. The truth is that belligerent personalities and stubbornly held opinions, then as now, resulted in division and hurt. Why is this the case in a group that should be characterized by love?

Perhaps selfishness and inflexibility are more pronounced in spiritual matters because they are so closely tied to one's identity. Christianity promises a new identity, "the mind of Christ" replacing the many minds of stubborn individuals. But when one considers the history of Christianity, the mind of Christ is all too often not evident. It may be realistic, then, to consider the concept a hopeless ideal. On the other hand, what would history have looked like if there had not been so many people trying, perhaps pitifully, to achieve unity in the name of Christ? But, however we may view the past, it is still possible to look for a better future, and it is essential in that regard to consider unity as the New Testament writers envisioned it.

THE SOURCE OF UNITY

We observed in the previous chapter that sympathy must begin with imagination, and imagination is aided by an appreciation for the suffering love of God himself. Unity is the next step in the progression of love. When one is enabled to bear the burden of another, something is shared that once belonged to one (or to two at separate times). Paul makes this sharing the basis of oneness in Philippians 2:1–2:

> So if there is any encouragement in Christ, any incentive of love, any participation in the Spirit, any affection and sympathy, complete my joy by being of the same mind, having the same love, being in full accord and of one mind. (RSV)

Essentially his argument is this: "If you have been given love by God, and if you have been able to give that love to each other, you ought to know unity." This may seem simplistic until we consider some of the attempts of well-meaning people to find a starting point for unity. Some people stress submission to personal or institutional authority, others stress majority vote, and still others stress consensus on doctrinal and behavioral standards. These may be part of the outgrowth of unity, but they are not its basis. The truth is more simple and therefore more profound: the necessary condition for unity is nothing more nor less than shared pain.

The New Testament offers a powerful reminder of this in the shared meal known as the Lord's Supper. It is the one and only holiday that believers are commanded to observe, and we are told to do it on a recurrent basis, together. And what do we do in this single required institutionalization of belief, in this one prescribed expression of unity? We feast on a dead body. The dead body of our own Victim, no less. That is what he tells us to do, and he tells us that we cannot live without this terrible food and this terrible drink.

We are reluctant cannibals. We prefer Christmas and Easter, when we can each enjoy our own piece of chocolate. But in this holiday, the holiday begun by Jesus, we are forced to look around at the others who have pieces of the same dismembered body in their hands, the same blood on their lips. It is an ugly image, but that is just the point. And it only makes it uglier to serve it up on silver dishes—as if cannibals could change the menu by changing their table manners. By participating in this meal, we only render ourselves ridiculous by looking away from the horror of it. By eating and drinking, we are forced to consider pain, our part in causing it, and God's cost in tranforming it. Paul writes that by doing this, over and over again, together, we "proclaim the Lord's death until he comes" (1 Cor 11:26). If you want to be *one*, you must begin with pain. God's pain. Then your pain. And then those faces around the table will begin to look different, and the idea of unity will begin to be a passion and not a chore.

THE MEANING OF "MIND"

To desire unity is to begin to ask seriously what it will look like when it begins to occur. An obvious question with which to begin is the question of the extent of unity. How much room is there for individual expression, privacy, disagreement, ownership, and decision? Granting that any description of oneness will certainly be part of a goal toward which we strive, how "one" will we be if we achieve it? We must begin by attempting to understand the vocabulary of unity in the New Testament.

When Paul urges the Philippians to be of "one mind," he does not use the word for "mind" that is usually used to denote intellect. That word is used in Luke 24:45, where it is said that Jesus "opened their minds so they could understand the Scriptures," or in Romans 14:5, where Paul recommends that in debatable matters, "each one should be fully convinced in his own mind." The word used in Philippians is also translated "mind," but in New Testament usage it is broader than, or prior to, the exercise of the intellect. It is usually used when the reference is to the outlook, the attitude, the mindset.[2] Thus when Paul warns the Romans not to be "high-minded" (Rom 11:20; 12:16 KJV), he is recommending a humble attitude, not a lack of knowledge. Similarly, when he contrasts the mind set on the Spirit with the mind set on the flesh (Rom 8:5–7, 27; cf. Phil 3:19; Col 3:2), he is recommending a predilection toward obedience, not merely *thought about* the Spirit.

Paul follows his explanation of the crucial "ethic of striving" with the command to be "thus minded" (Phil 3:15 RSV)—that is, to view the Christian life as a journey toward a

---

[2]The distinction should not, however, be oversimplified. There are a few instances of overlapping: Romans 1:28 and 1 Corinthians 1:10; 2:16 appear to use the first word (*nous*) to denote attitude, and 1 Corinthians 13:11 appears to use the second word (*phronein*) to denote intellectual activity.

goal. So it is that when he commands believers to be "like-minded" (Phil 2:2; cf. Rom 15:5), Paul is considering not a shared system of thought or moral code but a shared *orientation*. This orientation, as we will observe, must necessarily include some particulars of doctrine and conduct. But it is fundamentally a way of looking at life. And that, while more vague than some might hope, is yet more freeing than some might fear. It places the stress on celebration of what we share rather than on resolution of our points of difference. With this understanding, Paul's opening affirmation in Philippians takes on a new significance as a positive expression of unity:

> I thank my God every time I remember you. In all my prayers for all of you, I always pray with joy because of your partnership in the gospel from the first day until now, being confident of this, that he who began a good work in you will carry it on to completion until the day of Christ Jesus. It is right for me to feel this way about all of you, since I have you in my heart; for whether I am in chains or defending and confirming the gospel, all of you share in God's grace with me. God can testify how I long for all of you with the affection of Christ Jesus (Phil 1:3–8, my translation).

CHARACTERISTICS OF THE FIRST FELLOWSHIP

How will this shared orientation express itself in action? The early chapters of Acts contain two concise descriptions of the early community, of a time when "all the believers were one in heart and mind" (Acts 4:32). In Acts 2:42, Luke describes the *activities* of the very first group of converts: "They devoted themselves to the apostles' teaching [cf. 4:33] and to the fellowship, to the breaking of bread and to prayer" (cf. 2:46). He goes on to report that they "had everything in common" (2:44; cf. 4:32–35). These details were certainly intended by Luke as instruction, not merely information, for his readers; and so it is fair to read his description of "what was" as a description of "what ought to be." In other words, believers living in unity ought to (1) seek deeper understanding of their faith, (2) spend a great amount of time together, (3) share meals, (4) pray together, and (5) provide for the material needs of poorer believers.

This list offers a severe critique to most Christian groups today, and it makes it easy to understand the lack of unity within and between modern groups. The first and fourth items on the list appear to be covered by the worship service or by small-group activities. But all too often believers are brought to a certain level of knowledge and prayer—and then are left there, because this is the common denominator of the whole group, the level at which the greatest number are least threatened. As a plateau is reached, knowledge is stifled and prayer is depersonalized. Excitement and intimacy are denied, and boredom sets in. How can a group in such a situation hope to move toward oneness? If it moves at all, the group grows inward upon itself, and as a result there are petty quarrels. As with an ingrown toenail, the affliction goes unnoticed until infection is already advanced.

The third item on the list, shared meals, is at first glance covered by church "social activities." But anyone who knows the difference between an evening with close friends and an evening "entertaining" as a professional obligation will agree that unity cannot be produced by an enjoyable activity. Rather, enjoyable activities are produced by unity. How sad, moreover, that the level of conversation at church functions is often no more meaningful than that at a business luncheon: participants merely avoid profanity and begin the meal with a prayer of thanks for the food. What passes for "fellowship" here is in danger of being only a retreat from the pressure of dealing with "outsiders." This should be no more satisfying to the believer seeking unity than it would be physically satisfying to sit down in front of the food without eating it.

Would it be comforting at that moment to reassure oneself that the food at some other table is likely to be bad for one's health?

Sharing possessions, the fifth item on the list, is unusual in modern churches in developed countries. Few believers in Western countries are needy. Government social agencies provide what in other times and places are provided by individuals. Most churches have funds for emergency aid and attempt to distribute such monies equitably. Consequently, the behavior of the church in Acts is often brushed over as a noble but largely irrelevant example.[3] Such a conclusion demonstrates acute near-sightedness. There are needy believers by the millions in the Third World whose faint cries for help reach believers in the West only through the efforts of a few understaffed relief agencies. These agencies provide a few more appeals in the long list of potential recipients of our charity—and not very slickly packaged ones at that. But there is a clear biblical mandate to attend to the physical needs of other believers (e.g., Matt 25:34–46; Gal 6:10). In fact, there is a little-known example of precisely this behavior later in Acts (11:27–30): when believers in Antioch learned of a coming widespread famine, "each according to his ability, decided to provide help for the brothers living in Judea." Why should they send this aid over a long distance at some risk to people they did not know? Because the Judeans needed it, presumably worse than the Antiochenes did. Why should they not distribute aid to the needy in general in the vicinity of Antioch? Because, realistically, for unity to be meaningful, it must be selective. To express solidarity with one's fellows, even one's unknown fellows, *especially* one's unknown fellows,

---

[3]Some even go so far as to say that it was a bad idea, that the "divestiture of capital" was foolish from a business standpoint, and that the New Testament mentions such "communism" nowhere else. Both objections, however, must face directly the clear portrayal in the text of this sharing as admirable behavior.

sends a worthy challenge to the world: "Only God's power is able to make strangers into family—will you take what he offers?" Jesus himself made this the fundamental test of legitimacy: "By this all men will know that you are my disciples, if you love *one another*" (John 13:35; cf. 1 John 2:16–17; 4:20).

There is another item on the list of behaviors characteristic of the life of the first church. The believers spent a great amount of time together. This is not stated in exactly these words, but it is clearly implied by the shared activities described. There is probably no modern correspondent to this feature. In fact, believers today are often concerned that they spend too much time together when "there is a world out there to win." In reaction to the accusation that they might be sheltered, even cloistered, most want to spend as much time as possible "on the front lines," infiltrating the prevailing culture with the lifestyle and message of Christianity. This is admirable, and it might be argued that the apparently contrary picture in Acts describes only the initial response to the Gospel, which was in fact a preparation period for a later scattering. But there is cause for caution here. The bonds of trust typical of friendships, marriages, families, even good business associations, all depend on significant amounts of *shared time*. Shared time alone is not sufficient, but it is crucial. How could this be less true when we are grounding relationships that promise to go on *forever*?

THE LIMITS OF COMMUNITY

The example of the Acts community leads us to ask how far this idea of community should be or can be taken. Just how responsible are believers for each other? How much room is there for independence?

Paul thinks of the community of believers as an organism, a body (1 Cor 12:12–26; Eph 4:15–16), and he advances several insights implied by this metaphor. In a body, individual organs serve distinct but equally necessary functions. A wounded portion cannot be ignored or cut off—it must be helped. The whole body functions effectively only when the parts are directed and coordinated from the head, which is Christ.

Paul uses the body image to combat pride among those body parts with more visible functions and to discourage division initiated by those who feel "uncoordinated." This approach leaves very little room for independence and suggests enormous responsibility for others on the part of each person. This all sounds very good, but is it realistic, especially in our individualistic culture, to expect that many people will take such responsibility? Unfortunately, this may bring us back full circle to the opening paragraph of the chapter, to the suggestion that unity may be a hopeless ideal. In this area of striving toward obedience, pessimism about "arriving" may be more easily justified than in any other area. For the difficulty in this case is multiplied by the number of people in any group, each of whom brings a new arsenal of weaknesses and vices to contend with. Think of the power that is required for just two people to build a healthy marriage. Is it any wonder, then, that most believers give up on coordinated effort and leave the bulk of the work to paid professionals? And is it any wonder, following from that, that the "bulk" is so small, the historical record so embarrassing? This is discouraging, not because God has so little power to put at believers' disposal but rather because the believer exercises so much power to resist unity.

WHAT UNITES US, WHAT DIVIDES US

What progress we can make toward unity must begin with an understanding of what we do and do not share. For this purpose (and some others) the telephone directory is helpful.

My city directory lists about ninety Christian churches, and over half of these would describe themselves as evangelical. The mainline Protestant and Roman Catholic people know that the evangelicals often use terms like *Bible-believing, born again,*and *Spirit-filled,*but beyond this most are as incapable of distinguishing the groups from one another as the local nonchurchgoing majority is of distinguishing Jesus from Jim Jones.

As for the members of the evangelical congregations themselves, the picture is hardly more encouraging. No fewer than thirty distinct denominations are listed. But probably only a tiny handful (and not necessarily the ministers) could give a coherent explanation of a single doctrinal point that distinguishes their denomination from one listed on the next page of the directory. Fewer still are able to trace historically the division of their group from another. Although occasional mergers occur,[4] the tendency of these groups is to split and split again into ever more finely distinguished subgroups.

The point here is not to demean those courageous people who often pay a high personal price to facilitate revitalization by beginning anew when rigid institutions have "quenched the Spirit." Rather, the point is to challenge the assumption that the divisions of the past are legitimate for the present. Today, decisions about a church with which to affiliate for worship are made largely on the basis of *comfort*, not doctrine. Those who are willing to admit their ignorance of substantial differences will still say, "That group may not be *wrong*, but I just do not feel *comfortable* with them." To what extent is this legitimate?

---

[4]The Northern and Southern Presbyterians recently merged a mere hundred and twenty years after dividing over the slavery issue. Some Mennonite groups have combined after recognizing that splits in different countries at different times produced groups that differed in name only.

Some feel comfortable with a church that offers a familiar style of worship, perhaps because of family history. Others look for stimulating preaching, a convenient location, programs for children, or commitment to social concerns. Nearly everyone chooses (but not consciously) to be surrounded by people of similar social and economic status: some churches are clearly for the concert-hall crowd, others for bowling-league buddies. And even if the the church is economically mixed, the social groups within it rarely are. This orientation toward comfort may be acceptable if it can be admitted sheepishly, even jokingly, as the first step toward progress. But such comfort is dangerous when, as is so often the case, it encourages those who are comfortable with one another to conclude that their group is *different* in some significant way. This leads too easily to the conclusion that the group is *correct*. In two quick, unconscious steps, comfort becomes pride.

The denominational loyalist may be put off by the implications of this discussion. It is one thing to talk of unity, but actually to consider *acting* as one body—that is an *uncomfortable* thought! After all, tolerance can lead to compromise on important points (even if we are not sure what or how important they are), and compromise can lead to loss of identity (even though the world can scarcely identify the group except when members do things to embarrass the cause of Christ).

It seems simplistic to bring in the New Testament at this point. Its writers were not reducing the church from ninety groups to one but building from zero to one. And even if they were reducing, the splinter groups had not had time to become institutions. Nevertheless, words that were originally intended to address a simpler situation may serve as a powerful prophetic call today:

> As a prisoner for the Lord, then, I urge you to live a life worthy of the calling you have received. Be completely humble and gentle; be patient, bearing with one another in love. Make every effort to keep the unity of the Spirit through the bond of peace. There is one body and one Spirit—just as you were called to one hope when you were called—one Lord, one faith, one baptism; one God and Father of all, who is over all and through all and in all. (Eph 4:1–6)

These are the truths that unite believers. It is difficult to find in these words any basis for division, even though there is certainly room for disagreement over the finer details of definition among those who work humbly toward thorough understanding.

WORKING ON UNITY

How can believers reapproach unity today? What forms will their striving take? I can offer a few specific suggestions, not as requirements, but as invitations to the reader to *join with other believers* in creating and enacting such ideas. Churches could, for example, plan *regular* cross-denominational preaching, teaching, services, small-group studies, and social gatherings. Social services and occasional special events are not enough. Families could consider changing denominations if they relocate, and they could plan periodic visits to other churches. Those with teaching gifts should familiarize believers with fair explanations of historical and doctrinal roots of division and unity. These teachers should be aware of the danger that such explanations too often take the form of pointing out the mistakes of others. A last—but not least—suggestion is that Western churches should develop a *thorough* knowledge of, and support for, sister churches in other parts of the world, especially in developing countries.

These suggestions should provide a challenge, not a

threat. All of the efforts and activities I have suggested (and many more) could be done without structurally or doctrinally modifying our current denomination system. But by the power of God, that modification may be next.

Service:

"Submit Yourselves to One Another"

"**M**ay I clean your toilet?" How often has this offer been made this week by your Christian friends? Not often, I suspect.

In the ancient world, there were no toilets as we know them, so of course the offer was never made. But there may have been an equivalent. Given the condition of roads, the quality of footwear, and the level of personal sanitation, we can well imagine the reaction of embarrassed shock when the Deliverer of the Jewish Nation demanded to wash the feet of his followers:

> "No," said Peter, "you shall never wash my feet."
> Jesus answered, "Unless I wash you, you have no part with me."
> "Then, Lord," Simon Peter replied, "not just my feet but my hands and my head as well!" . . .
>
> When he had finished washing their feet, he put on his clothes and returned to his place. "Do you understand what I have done for you?" he asked them. "You call me 'Teacher' and 'Lord,' and rightly so, for that is what I am. Now that I, your Lord and Teacher, have washed your feet, you also should wash one another's feet. I have

set you an example that you should do as I have done for you." (John 13:8–9, 12–15; cf. Matt 20:28)

If this is to be more than a ritual, what will it mean in terms of day-to-day conduct? Must I literally, or even figuratively, live with other people's dirt under my fingernails?

LEADERS, RIGHTS, AND LOVE

The word *leadership* sells like nothing else in the marketing of education today. Even though every ladder-climbing executive must learn at least as much about performing for those above as about directing those below, no university could expect to attract students with the slogan, "We'll teach you to submit effectively." Christian organizations that advertise training in "servant-leadership" do not remedy this popular appeal to the will to power. What they produce are rarely leaders as the world recognizes leaders, and they are hardly servants as the Bible describes servants. So why use either word? We must squarely face the fact that the thought of service, except as a token or temporary activity, is distasteful. To accept a lower place is bad enough, but to *choose* a lower place—preposterous!

Words like *obey, submit, serve,* or worse, the expression "know your place," are met with defiance from a people who are obsessed with their "rights." Of course these rights are not wrong, and it is appropriate that there is legislation to protect rights. The problem is that legislation can only protect us from the bad; it cannot produce good in us. And it certainly cannot suggest to us that there might be some value in renouncing our rights for something or someone else. The Cross is the best evidence that there is much more to love than justice, much more to right than *rights.* A person who has won a public battle for human rights has done a good thing. But a person who has won a personal battle and given up human rights in the interest of human obligation has done a great thing. More often than not, the action will be labeled demeaning or ridiculous. So was the Cross. But the similarity is not always helpful when it comes to our own behavior. The Cross one can appreciate at a safe distance. Or Mother Theresa, or a kind grandmother, or one's own dear mother. Expressions of admiration can be a form of insulation from the heat of another's love, and the closer that person is the thicker we must lay it on. The same is true of applause for inspirational speakers: if we cannot relieve the tension of conviction by clapping, we might have to relieve it by *responding*. "Dear children," pleads the apostle John, "let us not love in words or tongue but with actions and in truth" (1 John 3:18).

SERVING IN THE NEW TESTAMENT

John precedes the plea just quoted with these words: "If anyone has material possessions and sees his brother in need but has no pity on him, how can the love of God be in him?" (1 John 3:17)

The most common and probably the most basic form of service in the New Testament is generosity with material possessions. It is basic because everyone has something to give. The fact of the gift, not its size, is crucial. No particular talent is required. The only serious danger is that such giving might be intended to buy favors from others or from God. But when the focus is on the need of the other or the affection felt for the other, this danger is minimized.

The New Testament is filled with examples of the service of generosity (e.g., Acts 9:36–39; Rom 15:25–31; 2 Cor 8:9), perhaps the most famous of which is the prostitute who washed and anointed the feet of Jesus (Luke 7:36–50; cf. Mark 14:3–9). This is a notable example of something not unusual during the ministry of Jesus. In the background as he traveled was a group of women who provided financial and domestic support to the group (Mark 15:40; Luke 8:1–3). Some of these same women, on their way to perform another "menial" service—to anoint the dead body of Jesus—were the first witnesses to the Resurrection. God has a sense of humor. We can imagine the delight of a host of angels (who, incidentally, exist only as servants [Heb 1:14]), leaning over the balcony of heaven, in on the joke, waiting for these trudging menials to arrive at the scene of the most important event in history. God's punchline, as usual, is the exaltation of those who lower themselves, those who serve. Heaven still rings, and ever will, with the laughter.

The vocabulary of service indicates that the concept is broader than material generosity. The word *deacon* is simply the transliteration of the Greek word for "servant." Originally the deacons' function was to distribute food in order to free up the apostles' time (Acts 6:1–6). Gradually their qualifications became more precise (1 Tim 3:8–13), and we observe people performing various or unspecified tasks who are called deacons (e.g., Phoebe [Rom 16:2] and Tychicus [Col 4:7–9]). "Serving" ("deaconing") is mentioned in two of three New Testament lists of "spiritual gifts": necessary functions in the community of believers for which God provides people who are uniquely suited to perform those functions (Rom 12:7; 1 Peter 4:11). In the third passage, Paul uses the more general meaning of the word, in the sense that the use of any gift of God is service (1 Cor 12:5). In this sense Paul often calls himself a servant/deacon (e.g., 1 Cor 3:5; 2 Cor 6:4; Eph 3:7) and his work a service (sometimes translated "ministry" [2 Cor 4:1; 1 Tim 1:12; 2 Tim 4:11]). The thread running through all of these texts is the idea of service as a freely offered activity, usually something commonplace, that benefits or boosts other believers.

SERVICE "VERSUS" SUBMISSION

I chose to address the subject of service first not only because it is so common and so basic but also because it paves the way for a more difficult subject: submission. One aspect of the New Testament teaching that is crucial to observe is that when this subject of service is discussed, the focus is always on the one who acts freely for the good of another, not on one who gives or follows orders. And as in so many areas of prescribed conduct, it is God himself who sets the pattern. Paul, while addressing an issue of church order, makes an instructive remark: he says that the head of man in general is Christ and the head of Christ is God (1 Cor 11:3). First consider the second part of this formula. When one reads the Gospels, one hardly gets the impression that when Jesus does the will of his Father (e.g., John 6:38), he is taking orders. No, he knows how to serve his Father, because he has been taught by his Father (John 8:28)—in other words, because they are one (John 14:10–11). Even at the decisive moment in the Garden of Gethsemane, he does not respond, "Oh, well, all right" to a commanding voice from heaven; rather, he volunteers the words "Yet not what I will, but what you will" (Mark 14:36). His submission is an offering, not a response.

Applying this in the arena of human relationships will mean taking initiative in doing good for others. When the words *kind* or *kindness* are used in the New Testament, this is what is meant (Gal 5:22; Eph 4:32; Col 3:12). Similarly, the words *good* or *goodness* (Matt 20:15 KJV; Gal 5:22; 6:6–10) and *honor* (Rom 12:10; 1 Tim 5:17; 1 Peter 3:7 RSV) often connote charitable initiative. There are those people who often ask, "Is there anything I can do?" Then there are those people who simply *do* what they can. A meal served, an errand run, a message delivered, an object lent or given—these are examples of the intentional service that is essential to submission. If I could produce a new word here, it would be *submitiative*.

OBEYING AS SUBMITTING

Offering obedience to another person is no problem in a situation where both parties are fulfilling indisputable roles, as for example when parents, policemen, or employers give reasonable directions within their realms of authority. Most New Testament commands to obey or submit to other people are covered by these examples.[1] The problems come either when the role is disputed (*"You* have no authority over me") or when the directions are not within the accepted realm of authority ("You have no authority over me *in this matter"*). Whenever the subject of obedience comes up, we imagine violations of either principle: office underlings giving orders to co-workers, governments like Hitler's making a policy of atrocities, etc. The New Testament is very clear with regard to "realm of authority." Any order that would violate God's law need not be obeyed. People should not be feared when they threaten unjustly (Matt 10:26–28; Acts 4:19; 1 Peter 3:13–15), but only when they command what they have a right to command (Mark 12:17; Rom 13:1–7; 1 Peter 2:13–20). This, of course, becomes less clear-cut when issues like the morality of war or "the spirit of the law" are introduced. With regard to "disputation of role," the New Testament offers no instruction. Roles may have been more clear then; or, more likely, the difficulties are too situation-specific to allow for helpful advice, either in New Testament books or in this one. Instead, each particular situation calls for wisdom, sensitivity, and dependence on God for guidance.

---

[1]Romans 13:1; Ephesians 6:1, 5; Colossians 3:20, 22; 1 Timothy 3:4; Titus 2:5, 9; 3:1; 1 Peter 2:13, 18. Uncomfortable though the terms may be, the principle of master-slave relations applies in most modern employment situations, so I include these texts.

RANK AND ROLE IN MARRIAGE

Both disputation of role and realm of authority are problems in marriage. It seems arbitary always to award precedence or rank to the male in this relationship, whatever tradition may dictate. And even if rank is granted, how far does it extend?

There can be no doubt that biblical authors lived contentedly in a male-dominated world, and there is no indication that they expected things to change until the Age of Promise, when the absence of marriage (Matt 22:30) will make the issue irrelevant. Indeed, a quick reading of the instruction to women[2] creates the impression that unquestioning obedience to husbands was expected. Without attempting to summarize or respond to the vast literature on this subject, I will offer some softening of this seemingly harsh picture that is not immediately obvious to the casual reader.

With one exception, which I will consider below, the word used in addressing the wife is "submit," not "obey." As we have seen, this word has a broader and more positive connotation than "obey." It is especially interesting to observe that in the Ephesians and Colossians passages "obey" is used when addressing children (Eph 6:1; Col 3:20) and slaves (Eph 6:5; Col 3:22), but "submit" is used when addressing wives. Clearly there was a more (I do not say fully) egalitarian conception of the marriage relationship that called for a distinction in terms.

The instruction to believers in Ephesians 5–6 begins in verse 21 with the command, "Submit to one another out of reverence for Christ." The fact that instruction to wives and husbands immediately follows does not mean that mutual submission in marriage is commanded here; rather, Paul is

---

[2]Wives must submit to their husbands: Ephesians 5:22–24; Colossians 3:18; Titus 2:5; 1 Peter 3:1–6; wives must submit to the church: 1 Corinthians 11:2–16; 14:33–35; 1 Timothy 2:11–15.

introducing the entire "house table," or list of instructions to each member of the household. Verse 21 could therefore be paraphrased, "Each of you has someone else to whom you should submit." The implication of verse 23, "Christ is the head of the church" (along with 1 Cor 11:3) is that the husband as head of the household is answerable to God. This idea, combined with the radical commands for the husband to give himself for his wife (v. 25), nourish and cherish her (v. 29), and love her as he loves himself (v. 33) define the husband's awesome realm of responsibility. He is told to treat her as Christ treats his followers, and everything that is commanded in the passage is consistent with the activity of Jesus as described earlier in this book. Nowhere is the husband told to *rule* his wife; rather, taking Christ as his model, he is to *serve* her. The last command in the passage is for the wife to fear (NIV "respect") her husband. This is, of course, an appropriate fear of the consequences of wronging an authority that is operating within its realm (cf. Rom 13:3–4).

The New Testament does not spell out the wife's realm of authority, but the picture of an ideal wife familar to New Testament era believers from the Book of Proverbs destroys the insecure male's caricature of the wife as a simpering homebody. A good wife, according to Proverbs 31, works long hours to provide for the household (v. 15), delegates authority to her staff (v. 15), buys and sells property (vv. 16–18), dispenses charity (v. 20), and teaches wisdom to the family (vv. 25–26). She is no charmer, no beauty (v. 30), but she is a marvel of productive competence. If this description contains anything demeaning, to modern eyes, it is the description of her husband, who appears to spend much of his time at the club, bragging her up (vv. 23, 28, 31).

The only passage that uses "obey" as an address to wives is 1 Peter 3:1–6, where wives are commanded to "be submissive" (vv. 1, 5), and Sarah is cited as an example: she "obeyed Abraham and called him her master" (v. 6). Here the instruction to women to dress modestly and to possess "a gentle and quiet spirit" (v. 4) sounds unreasonable to many women: why not lay the same charge to the men? A bit of history may help here.[3] Roman writers of the time indicate an assumption (based on a mix of fact and suspicion) that women involved in pagan cults were sexually promiscuous. Flashy clothing was worn in some cult rituals, and any separation from the religion of the husband was a form of defiance. These two factors fed the flames of suspicion. The question for Peter, writing to Christian women with nonbelieving husbands, was this: how can these men be convinced that *this* new religion does not involve sexual infidelity? His proposal: avoid dress and behavior that might allow him to associate you with the cults. This is consistent with Peter's other teaching about anticipation of persecution (2:12, 16; 3:16; 4:14–16), and it accounts neatly for his specific instructions.

All of this is not to suggest that first-century Christians knew of egalitarian marriages, but it does suggest that the biblical view of marriage roles is not as unfairly one-sided as some feminists accuse and some husbands wish. Modern equivalents to the functions of the Proverbs 31 woman allow for significant access to power in the relationship on the part of the wife, and the availability of education to women justifies movement away from the model that was appropriate in that ancient culture. Knowledge is and was power, and in that world almost all women were illiterate. In any case, common sense dictates that modern couples agree in detail about rank and role expectations *before* entering marriage.

---

[3]This explanation is documented in a technical monograph by D. L. Balch, *Let Wives Be Submissive: The Domestic Code in 1 Peter* (Chico, Calif., 1981).

Within that context of agreement, biblical principles of submission and obedience will be much easier to apply.

SUBMISSION AND CHURCH LEADERS

Christian leaders today, Protestant and to a lesser extent Catholic, can easily understand what was once said of someone's cat: "My cat never *obeys* me; sometimes it *agrees* with me." Whatever combination of factors has led to the decline in awe of spiritual directors, the fact is that obedience to a human authority in the church is foreign to most people. We procure input from authorities and then do what they recommend because we *agree* with it, not because *they* recommend it.

Paul names some church leaders who had "devoted themselves to the service of the saints," and he goes on, "I urge you, brothers, to submit to such as these and to everyone who joins in the work, and labors at it." (1 Cor 16:15–16; cf. 2 Thess 3:14). Similarly, the author of Hebrews commands, "Obey your leaders and submit to their authority. They keep watch over you as men who must give an account" (Heb 13:17). As early as the first decades of the second century, extensive authority was granted to church leaders who were to be obeyed "as the Lord himself" (Ignatius to the Ephesians, c. 115 A.D.). The Protestant reaction to this and subsequent developments in the church limits the realm of authority of a church leader, but many are comfortable with the idea of being taught and advised, or "discipled" by one who is "older in the Lord." This is simply a loosely structured rendition of the Roman Catholic concept of the "spiritual director," and these are both in turn attempts to follow the pattern of discipleship under Jesus hinted at in the Gospels. The fact that the authority passed on by him to his disciples (Matt 16:18–19) is inevitably tainted by their shortcomings makes it difficult to recognize them as true authorities or to grant them any but the most narrow realm of authority. The closer we get to our spiritual leaders, the less we see them as examples. On the other hand, we cannot follow them at a distance. We lose the trail in the snow and wind of mere words. It is so much easier just to stand where we are and admire them where (we imagine) they are. The distance is comfortable for both. It is painful to cross that space.

Nevertheless, it may be just at this point, where our most central selves are affected, that submission reaches out as far as it can—and finds that the space is not empty, but that another Hand reaches back. For it is in treating another weak person as if that person were *Jesus*—not only to serve, but even to obey—that we make ourselves most vulnerable, most embarassing, most like the One who would clean his friends' toilets.

· 8 ·

Verbal Nurture:
"Build Each Other Up"

W hy, instead of explaining his teachings, did Jesus tell so many stories? His use of parables to convey life-changing truths is one of several important aspects of his career that have no parallel in antiquity. Jews were familiar with the riddle or metaphor used occasionally to make a point, but here was a man who spoke of the most important matters and answered the most incriminating questions *in stories*. Why? We normally think of storytellers as warm, folksy types. But the life and death issues in the parables do not admit a view of Jesus as an Aesop or an Uncle Remus. Entertainers—even bad ones—do not end up on crosses.

The key to understanding the unusual approach of Jesus may be found in the invitation that ends many of the parables: "He who has ears to hear, let him hear." The point is this: the very nature of a parable allows the hearer to take an active part in the hearer's own persuasion. The parable is in this sense a mark of humility on the part of the speaker, a message of respect toward the listener. In a larger and more important sense, each of the Gospels is in itself a parable. God, in humility and respect—in a word, in *love*—invites each of us to have ears to hear. The story is difficult. It reveals; it conceals. One must work out its significance. How like God: he offers a puzzle to which he is the key, a riddle to which he is the answer.

For God, then, words are not trivial. It is through words—indeed, through the Word himself, Jesus—that God coaxes us into the truth and the implications of his love. To take our own words seriously, therefore, is to take seriously God's words to us.

In A.D. 108, Ignatius, bishop of Antioch, was condemned for his loyalty to Jesus and sent to Rome to be torn apart by wild beasts. He wrote several farewell letters, in one of which he wrote about Jesus' example of combining action with words:

> It is better to be silent and be real than to talk and not be real. To teach is good if the teacher also acts. There is one Teacher who spoke and it was done, and what he did in silence is worthy of the Father. He who truly possesses the word of Jesus can also hear his silence. This will lead to his perfection: to action consistent with words, to communication even in silence.

Talk is cheap, but its effect can be very costly. Ignatius is long dead, his wisdom unheeded. Today a torrent of Christian advice and opinion flows from the notions of human equality, individual political rights, and the priesthood of all believers—often drowning out the slow, quiet voice of care. Mass communication has made the spoken word the means to power, especially when ideas are reduced to the level of slogans. Moderate or complex positions simply don't sell. The combination of personal charisma and effective propaganda, on the other hand, will sell almost anything. Consequently, words change their meaning as the people associated with them fall in or out of public favor. The somewhat related words *born-again*, *fundamentalist*, *evangelical*, and *televangelist*, for example, have recently become household words with largely negative connotations. Since so many are more interested in the people connected with the words than in the meaning of the words, only the use of still more *new words* will allow the people associated with the old ones to regain favor. We will have new slogans rather than careful definitions.

CAN WE TALK?

Faced with such confusion and the unlikelihood of a trend toward careful use of words, the believer might want to move in the direction of action without words. Certainly sympathy, unity, and service, the themes of the earlier chapters of this section, must come first. They are priorities in the literal sense of the word: they must come *prior* to talk. Otherwise the speaker is forced to maintain a distance from the audience, both public and private, and the destruction of the speaker is inevitable. The distance will produce either moral decline or ineffective communication—the only question is which will come first. One path ends in notoriety, the other in obscurity, but I suspect that the difference in the public eye is not important to God. The right to speak is won, for his perspective, by obedience.

Of course, not every audience hearing our advice or opinions is able to see that our behavior matches our words. Indeed, it would be bad behavior to tell them; furthermore, much good behavior is unobservable to all or to all but the few toward whom it is directed. "Your father who sees in secret" (Matt 6:4 RSV) knows, and every bit of advice or instruction must be empowered and tempered by the secrets, good and bad, shared only with him.

There is a place for talk, but it must be the most fearful responsibility of all those responsibilities to be fulfilled toward other believers. Unfortunately—and typically—we tend to reverse things. We are not in the least frightened by our own words. The fact is that our glib talk actually consoles us, because it makes us feel as if we have actually done what our talk implies. Actions, on the other hand, frighten us, because they imply the insufficiency or hypocrisy of our talk. They also remind us that we might do still more.

What we know about the authors of New Testament books suggests that they understood the proper sequence of action and speech. They did not write down theories of living in advance of living them. Instead, their writings were the product of their mature thought, built on lengthy experience. It is likely that their audiences were hungry for their words because they knew these men first as exemplary leaders. Paul, for example, did not write his earliest surviving letter until at least fifteen years, and his major works until about twenty-five years, after he began his work as an apostle.

The entire New Testament *is* the speaking that follows from the action of Paul and his fellow leaders. Every page is intended to instruct and ultimately to move believers toward greater love for God and neighbor. Even narrative sections are meant to be read this way. When we are told, for example, that the crowds wondered at the deeds of Jesus or that people followed him in discipleship, the implication is that the audience of the book should do the same. Scholarly scrutiny affirms this, but it is easy enough for anyone to surmise that men who were devoting their lives to such a cause would not write books merely to satisfy curiosity. They designed their communication not to inform so much as to transform.

IS NURTURE POSSIBLE?

How can one person's words, spoken or written, have an effect on the life of another? This is an important question, because the New Testament writers went beyond their own attempts at nurture to suggest that believers nurture one another.

The parables of Jesus, and his life as a parable, are an important method of nurture, as I noted before. God is creative enough to *intrigue* us. The result is that instead of being shackled to him, we embrace him. *The story*, then, whether in the form of illustration, creative fiction, or personal experience, encourages us to make our own connection and application. The story is perhaps the best way to convey sympathy when words are appropriate, and it is probably the worst way to convey advice in private conversation. It is hard to imagine anything more insensitive than the response, "Well, here is what I did [right] in that situation . . " The effort required to verbalize the pain or puzzlement of another by relating it to one's own pain or puzzlement, on the other hand, is in some situations the only way to demonstrate deep care.

Criticism, either positive or negative, functions as a sort of "second conscience" for most of us and is another important form of verbal nurture. It happens that I respond well to praise. It makes me want to live up to the commendation offered by another person. I do not respond well to censure. My tendency is to become defensive and discouraged. The sensitive critic will know which person and which occasion calls for a pat on the back, and which calls for a kick elsewhere.

Instruction functions to impart information, or more commonly, to combine truths in new and creative ways, in order to encourage agreement. Agreement with the truth of a matter is the first step toward active response, and we all require persuasion from time to time to stimulate us.

Meaningful conversation is yet another form of verbal nurture. Unlike the forms described above, it may not have a specific end in view, but it is nonetheless important because it is our most common opportunity to love in words. There are few people who are known for gentle speech, insightful questions, and conversation about things that matter. They tend not to say much, not because they have little to say, but because they have a hard time finding partners for their conversation. I have encountered a few such people, and I have found that the level of my own speech is drawn closer to their level—they seem immune to any negative effect from me. I doubt that this quality of speech came naturally to them, but having reached that level of verbal discipline, they have a natural effect on others.

It is important to understand the function of these several forms of verbal nurture before describing their place in the New Testament, because of all the behaviors described in this volume, the use of words is the one about which we are most likely to deceive ourselves. After all, we use lots of words. We tell stories of our personal experience, we criticize, we instruct, we discuss. The temptation is to suppose that with a little fine-tuning, we can move on to another, more challenging area of obedience. Unfortunately, though, our natural tendency is to use words as tools of manipulation, and until that orientation changes, our apparent mastery is a masquerade. The New Testament describes words as tools not of manipulation but of *construction*. Speech is for supporting, for putting pieces together, for elevating. The word *edify* and the Greek word for which it is a translation come from the building trade: to edify is to build up. Paul uses the word numerous times in 1 Corinthians 14 in his appeal to a church torn down by misuse of words, and he commonly uses it as a general reference to right conduct (Rom 14:19; Eph 4:11–16; 1 Thess 5:11). *Edify* occurs about twenty times in the New Testament; but the concept, specified in the forms of expression outlined above, occurs on practically every page. It is doubtless a dominant theme, then, that words must be instruments of construction.

PATS AND KICKS

The most common word used in the New Testament to denote strong verbal suggestion, often translated "exhort," is *parakaleō* (noun form: *paraklēsis*). Well-meaning preachers sometimes make much of the constituents of this compound word, which when taken literally suggest that one who exhorts is one who is "called alongside" another, especially as a comforter. This would of course provide wonderful linguistic support for the connection between sympathy and verbal nurture. But compound words were not understood as the sum of their parts in Greek any more than they are in English. If, for example, I say that I "understand" you, you do not glance down to see if I am standing beneath you. By considering the common use of the word at the time, it is clear that it was understood as the equivalent of our words *urge*, *appeal*, or even *beg*. The noun form is used about a dozen times in the sense of "comfort" in response to grief (Matt 5:4; 2 Cor 1:4; 1 Thess 3:7 RSV), but even these instances may be understood as appeals. For example, Paul describes the future hope of believers and concludes, "Therefore comfort one another *with these words*" (1 Thess 4:18 RSV, italics mine).

Another two dozen occurrences of *paraklēsis* and over a hundred occurrences of the verb *parakaleō* clearly connote verbal incitement to action. Paul frequently uses the word, urging believers to engage in a variety of general and specific behaviors. The sentence beginning "I appeal to you to" may be completed, for example, by the following requests:

. . . be subject to [your leaders] and to every fellow worker and laborer (1 Cor 16:16 RSV);

. . . arrange in advance for this gift you have promised, so that it may be ready not as an exaction but as a willing gift (2 Cor 9:5 RSV);

. . . lead a life worthy of the calling to which you have been called (Eph 4:1 RSV);

> ... that as you learned from us how you ought to live and to please God, just as you are doing, you do so more and more (1 Thess 4:1 RSV);
>
> ... do [your] work in quietness and to earn [your] own living (2 Thess 3:12 RSV).

Even more illustrative of Paul's style than these "one-liners" are his numerous extended appeals. He draws on his common experience with the community he addresses, his knowledge of the Scriptures, his training in classical rhetoric, and even his personal authority as an apostle to appeal for unity (1 Cor 1–4), belief in the resurrection (1 Cor 15), financial assistance (2 Cor 8–9), and freedom from legalism (Gal 1–6).

To those who will take from him the responsibility of community leadership Paul passes on the authority to make such appeals. Addressing himself to Timothy, a young church leader in Ephesus, he charges: "Preach the word, be urgent in season and out of season, convince, rebuke, and exhort, be unfailing in patience and in teaching" (2 Tim 4:2 RSV). That last clause, if remembered, is an effective check on the tendency to use words as a weapon of dominance. Peter voiced a similar and familiar appeal to communicate the faith: "Always be prepared to give an answer to everyone who asks you to give the reason for the hope that you have" (1 Peter 3:15). But this command is usually quoted without the adjoining clauses: "But do this with gentleness and respect, keeping a clear conscience ..." (3:16). The evidence is that the apostles embodied the powerful potential of such a charge. Paul and Peter, the two pillars of early church authority, stood on platforms held together only by their obedience to their own appeals.

CRITICISM AND DISCIPLINE

Commendation, the positive form of criticism, is common in the New Testament. The Beatitudes (Matt 5:3–12)

are the most familiar example of praise and promise for
righteousness, and it is significant that the first word in Jesus'
Sermon on the Mount is "blessed." Those who fit his
description would immediately feel affirmed; those who did
not would want to do what it takes to know the blessing.
Specific examples are plentiful. Imagine the feeling of the
centurion when Jesus, after seeing his faith, "was astonished
and said to those following him, 'I tell you the truth, I have
not found anyone in Israel with such great faith'" (Matt
8:10). Or think of the Romans' response when they read
Paul's words, "I thank my God through Jesus Christ for all of
you, because your faith is being reported all over the world"
(Rom 1:8). To the Philippians Paul wrote, "I always pray
with joy because of your partnership in the gospel" (Phil 1:4–
5). He called the Thessalonians "a model to all the believers"
and verbally wondered, "How can we thank God enough for
you in return for all the joy we have in the presence of our
God because of you?" (1 Thess 1:7; 3:9). I suspect that the
audiences of these and the many other words of praise in the
New Testament reacted as I might: "*You* think that of *me*?
God help me to act all the more in a way to deserve such
praise!"

There is frank censure in the New Testament as well.
Modern Christians are often shy to offer negative words, at
least to the one who merits them. It is so much "nicer" to
bury hatchets—in carefully marked places, where they can
be exhumed later. But the New Testament model suggests
that resolution must come *through* controversy, and it offers
specific guidelines for such resolution. The first principle is
immediate confrontation (Matt 5:21–26; 18:15). It is inevitable that people will be angry; the key is "Do not let the sun go
down while you are still angry" (Eph 4:26). When personal
confrontation fails, a group discussion is in order (Matt 18:16;
cf. 1 Tim 5:19). This helps to insure that the criticism is not
just a personal grudge. When small group confrontation fails,

and a serious behavioral matter is at issue, the authority of the local church must be exercised (Matt 18:17; 1 Cor 5:11–13; Titus 3:10–11). The ultimate discipline is exclusion from the body of believers, either until the person humbles himself (2 Thess 3:14–15) or, in more severe cases, perhaps for life (1 Cor 5:1–5).

The important principle here is that the most powerful gift of believers to one another is love, which requires time together to accomplish. This means that the exclusion, the withdrawal of that time together, is the most potent weapon at the disposal of the community of believers. Physical and economic violence are the domain of God (or at times the state). Believers, on the other hand, exercise the power of love. In Paul's day, of course, community membership was something that people counted a precious privilege, often at great risk to reputation or safety. Today local churches strive to make membership as comfortable and nonthreatening as possible, and as soon as someone begins to feel uncomfortable, there is another church down the street with open doors. And if one is uncomfortable there, television church or the ultimate individualization of faith—avoidance of community and accountability altogether—are popular options. Discipline in such circumstances is scarcely possible and rarely attempted. Only in those few places where individuals consent to accountability and their leaders fearfully accept this responsibility can it happen at all. The sad irony is that centuries of fighting and splitting have made communities of believers virtually immune structurally from the only means to preserve a strong unity: accountability *with teeth*.

INSTRUCTION

Everyone functions as a teacher for another person from time to time. But when a person takes on a position as dispenser of truth for a group, some checks and balances are in order. According to the New Testament, God gives as gifts to the church prophets, pastors, and teachers (Rom 12:3–8; 1 Cor 12:4–11; Eph 4:11–16). The simplest distinction between these is that prophets pass on messages directly from God whereas pastors and teachers convey their understanding of God's truth. Pastors (also called elders or bishops) are distinguished from teachers as leaders of worship and wielders of authority over community members (1 Tim 4–6). The responsibility, and the obvious temptation to claim messages or authority from God in order to manipulate others, requires careful scrutiny of such figures. The crucial qualification is that their lives match their words to the greatest possible extent (Matt 7:15–20; 1 Tim 4:11–12; 2 Tim 2:22–26; Titus 2:7–8). It is also essential that their teaching be in accordance with the Scriptures and the doctrine they received from their teachers (1 Cor 14:29; 2 Cor 11:1–6; 2 Tim 3:14–4:5). This requires maturity, training, and intelligence, and these qualities must be affirmed by leaders, not merely proclaimed by the hopeful instructor (1 Tim 4:14–15).[1]

Some of the greatest instruction to instructors occurs in the epistle of James. He advises, "Not many of you should presume to be teachers, my brothers, because you know that we who teach will be judged more strictly" (James 3:1). He goes on to describe the danger of the human tongue and concludes that the one who is "wise and understanding" among them should "show it by his good life, by deeds done in the *humility* that comes from wisdom" (James 3:13, italics mine). Wisdom as the world defines it is title, fame, and power. "But the wisdom that comes from heaven is first of all pure; then peace loving, considerate, submissive, full of mercy

---

[1] It is likely that the almost universal illiteracy of women during the New Testament era disqualified them from these functions (1 Cor 14:33–35; 1 Tim 2:12), but there were apparently a few exceptions to this rule (Acts 18:26; 21:9; perhaps Rom 16:1, 6, 12).

and good fruit, impartial and sincere" (James 3:17). The list of behaviors is remarkably similar to the Beatitudes (Matt 5:3–12) and the fruit of the Spirit (Gal 5:22–23), and its presence here reminds teachers that their function carries with it an even greater responsibility than that of other believers to represent the ideals that the teachers describe.

CONSTRUCTIVE CONVERSATION

The workplace and the home are the most common places for talk, and they are the places where we are least likely to be self-consciously well-behaved. Around those who know us well we set aside our masks. Sometimes in the name of "relaxation" or "being natural," we freely abuse those we care about, gossip shamelessly, and abandon common forms of courtesy. In a bizarre reversal of values, we reserve our best talk for strangers and "religious types" whom we would rather avoid.

A group of New Testament exhortations challenges this tendency:

> (Remind them) to speak evil of no one, to avoid quarreling, to be gentle, and to show perfect courtesy toward all men (Titus 3:2 RSV).

> Nor should there be obsenity, foolish talk or coarse joking, which are out of place, but rather thanksgiving (Eph 5:4).

> Let your conversation be always full of grace, seasoned with salt (Col 4:6).

> Whatever is true, whatever is noble, whatever is right, whatever is pure, whatever is lovely, whatever is admirable—if anything is excellent or praiseworthy—think about such things (Phil 4:8).

Conversation that edifies requires concentration, because it will involve resisting the desire to "fit in" to relationships and groups characterized by the abuse of words. Because obedience to God on this point can cost a friendship or a promotion, we might tend to think that, after all, silly talk and gossip are such small faults compared to theft or adultery—why pay such a high price for such a small thing? The answer, I think, is that it is not at all such a small thing. Paul suggested that the simple avoidance of "complaining and arguing" would mark believers as "blameless and pure, children of God without fault in a crooked and depraved generation, in which you shine like stars in the universe" (Phil 2:14–15). Why such high words for mere abstinence from grumbling? Try lasting a day without grumbling, and it will be clear how "mere" it really is. It may require far more of the power that God offers to perform such a feat than to resist "bigger" temptations. The latter do not present themselves often except in our imaginations anyway, and most of us at our worst are still held in check by cowardice. But destructive talk takes scarcely more effort than breathing. We do not give up breathing easily. Thus is it precisely these mundane little opportunities to transform words from destructive to constructive tools that mark us as transformed individuals. In our mouths these little words seem insignficant, but they enter the ears of others with a deafening roar: "Here is something truly powerful! Here is something truly good! Do *you* want it?"

Words of sympathy, appeal, praise, explanation, and peace transform worlds as large as the Roman Empire or as small as a family or a circle of friends. God set it all in mighty motion in the truth of the most powerful phrase ever penned: "The Word became flesh" (John 1:14).

Part III

The Believer in Relation to the World

Dear friends, I urge you, as aliens and strangers in the world, to abstain from sinful desires, which war against your soul. Live such good lives among the pagans that, though they accuse you of doing wrong, thay may see your good deeds and glorify God on the day he visits us.

1 Peter 2:11–12

• 9 •

Pain:

"It Is for Suffering That You Continue"

A friend came to our house yesterday, and in the course of our conversation she mentioned that things are not going well at all for her church. She paused, and my wife and I braced ourselves. "They are expanding the sanctuary," she continued. "It's terrible! The bathrooms don't work, and we have to go to the next building to get water for coffee!"

This heart-rending tale of the suffering church in late-twentieth-century America deserves no further comment. It does, however, introduce a question. Given the large amount of space in the New Testament devoted to suffering at the hands of hostile outsiders, is the New Testament in this sense out of step with our times? Or, worse, are believers today so conformed to the times that we are not distinct enough to merit hostility?

This chapter begins part 3, concerning the believer's relation to those outside the believing community. Pain is of course inflicted by diseases and accidents common to human experience, and in chapter 2 we considered the kind of relation to God that produces growth through such circumstances. But when the New Testament speaks of suffering, it is usually suffering incurred at the hands of others because of one's beliefs. This is probably so both because persecution was a particular affliction of believers in Christ and because such abuse provided a temptation to retaliate. It was important for those believers to understand the problem of persecution in terms of God's particular design and to learn what responses would edify both the abused individuals and their tormentors.

SUFFERING AS PURPOSE

One of the most startling statements in the New Testament occurs in the Epistle to the Hebrews. After recounting the sufferings for faith of believers in the past (chap. 11), the author points to Jesus as the best example of all, "who for the joy set before him endured the cross" (12:2). Then, after reminding his audience of the Old Testament teaching that God, like a good earthly father, disciplines those he loves, the writer makes this remarkable claim: "It is for discipline that you endure" (12:7 RSV). The word *endure* here can also be translated "persevere" or "continue [in the faith]." Together with the imagery of discipline in the context as "educational pain," we might paraphrase the statement in this way: "Continue as a believer for the purpose of educational pain." Can this be? Apparently so, as long as we are children of a loving Father. Nor is this the only explicit statement of this idea. In his first epistle Peter writes, "If you suffer for doing good and you endure it, this is commenadable before God" (2:20). He begins the next verse by saying, "For you have been called for this purpose" (NASB), and he goes on to describe Christ's example. Constructive suffering, or educational pain, is central to a life of faith.

The idea is expressed strongly by Paul as well. In Romans 8:17, he makes suffering the condition of eternal inheritance, calling believers "co-heirs with Christ, if indeed we share in his surrerings in order that we may also share in his glory." In Philippians 1:29 Paul writes that "it has been *granted* to you on behalf of Christ not only to believe in him, but also to suffer for him." (Italics mine.)

THE CIRCLE OF OBEDIENCE

While making such statements about the centrality of suffering, the New Testament writers are careful to avoid the implication that God is sadistic. Suffering leads somewhere. Paul, in Romans 5:3–5, puts it this way:

> We also rejoice in our sufferings, because we know that suffering produces perseverance; perseverance, character; and character, hope. And hope does not disappoint us, because God has poured out his love into our hearts by the Holy Spirit, whom he has given us (cf. 2 Cor 4:16–5:5).

These passages continue in the same manner. Hebrews 12:7 is followed in 12:11 by the reason for the centrality of suffering:

> No discipline seems pleasant at the time, but painful. Later on, however, it produces a harvest of righteousness and peace for those who have been trained by it.

Similarly, 1 Peter 2:20 is followed by a statement of the purpose of Christ's exemplary suffering: ". . . that we might die to sins and live for righteousness" (2:24).

Illustrations from our own times are not hard to find. For example, a businessman is attempting to follow Jesus in the way he conducts himself at work. His superiors ask him to falsify data for the sake of a client. He is cajoled, harassed, and finally insulted, but he refuses to participate in the questionable action. He accepts abuse in quiet confidence that he answers to Someone much higher on the Organizational Chart. The result? Admiration? Remorse on the part of his superiors, a new moral climate in the office? Hardly. Instead, he is passed over for promotion for not being a "team player."

The incident illustrates the idea that pain brings about the possibility of obedience, and obedience in its turn brings about the possibility of more pain. How will this businessman react now? There is a greater pain possible, and so there is a greater obedience possible. It is a circle. Or perhaps more precisely, it is a spiral, drawing the believer upward through suffering and obedience ever closer to the example of Jesus, ever closer to the character of God.

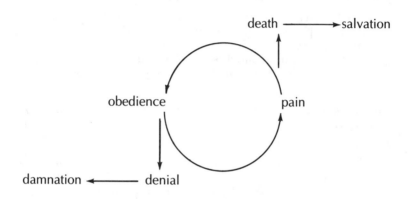

There are only two ways out. One way is to avoid pain, which sooner or later, and then to a greater and greater extent, will mean avoidance of God. For either he wants the pain or he wants to make use of the pain, and to reject it is to reject God. To deny the relation of pain to faith, then, is the ultimate disobedience.

The other way out of the circle is death, which is the the ultimate pain. This is another of God's ironic twists in the scheme of things. For in his way, death brings the ultimate deliverance from pain (salvation), whereas its avoidance in disobedience brings the ultimate deliverance *to* pain (damnation).

HOW PAIN WORKS

Suffering is constructive in several ways. For one thing, it constitutes *practice* in goodness. As Hebrews 5:14 puts it, the mature "have their faculties trained *by practice* to distinguish good from evil" (RSV, italics mine). In other words, they have formed habits through experience that enable them to make better decisions in new situations. The person who expects resistance to goodness from others is less likely to be caught off guard and to react resentfully toward others or toward God. Thus Peter advises, "Dear friends, do not be surprised at the painful trial you are suffering, as though something strange were happening to you" (1 Peter 4:12). A habitual and peaceful response results from expectation, and such expectation is far more likely to come from experience than from theory.

Pain also type-casts the believer. The command of Jesus to take up one's cross (Mark 8:34) was not to "bear a burden," as cross bearing is understood in popular speech today. Nor did it mean that all who followed Jesus would or should die a martyr's death. The distinctive feature of public executions, which survived until the last century, was the parade to the place of execution, lined by gawkers and especially mockers. The cross-bearing command of Jesus conveyed this idea: "Live in such a way that those who abuse me will abuse you, like a prisoner on the way to execution." It was a common theme of Jesus that hatred and abuse would accompany conformity to his way (Matt 5:11; Mark 13:13; John 15:18–21).

The result of this abuse is constructive in two ways. It produces social ostracism (1 Peter 4:1–5), which forces mutual reinforcement within the community. Believers are cast together by circumstances and have occasion to encourage one another. The need is felt far more acutely in the midst of social adversity than in the midst of social prosperity. More personally, the abuse produces a reputation that feeds itself.

In other words, once one is type-cast as a "goody-goody," it is hard to keep from living up to the reputation. "Oh, but *you* wouldn't want to go that party anyway." Once such statements begin, attempts to retreat to the comfort of conformity are worse than useless. People hate those who vacillate even more than they hate do-gooders, and the one who vacillates suffers most acutely from self-hatred.

In my own experience, the greatest constructive function of pain has been to "lift the veil." The very fact that I call myself a believer implies that I am not perfectly a *knower*. The great promise exists that I will one day know as I am known (1 Cor 13:12). But I cannot now *see* God, and my often foggy realization of his presence, my misty conception of his message, frustrates me. Am I merely imagining? It is as if there is a veil between me and God most of the time.

Two kinds of experience have lifted that veil for me. One is joy—that intense, simultaneous longing and satisfaction that God gives in those occasional moments when the weight of his love makes everything light. It is a very rare experience for me, and rightly so. My tendency would be to focus on the experience, to hold *it* against the dark of my doubts and temptations, to want *it* like an addict wants a drug—for what it gives, for the thrill. But I am called to live by faith in the Son of God, and to live by faith in what he *gives* is to choose destruction. It violates the first commandment, to have no other gods before God, no matter how like him they may appear. The fact that they "appear" at all—their contact with our senses, their *sensuality*—is in fact the first sign of danger. The veil is not being lifted; rather, a mask is being placed before it. I fear that many today take this subtle path away from God, and the lust for joy is a likely cause.

The other way that the veil is lifted is the way of pain. This is God's most effective method for most of us. It is in pain that I have been torn from my own supports—relational, economic, intellectual—and cast into . . . what? When all of these things are gone that comprise or at least prop up my identity, is that which remains outside of me a void or a Presence? My experience in such moments has been a powerful perception of affection, power, direction, and knowledge—within and without, nowhere in particular, and larger than everywhere. My senses were not affected, but they responded. The veil was gone. God was simply there. And I repeat that it was in moments of greatest loss that this great gain occurred. It is difficult to use language to convey a wordless presence. Ah, but God did that, too. Many times. Indeed, the greatest veil of all, the curtain in the temple symbolizing the separation of men from God's presence, was torn apart by the greatest pain of all, that of God's Son on the cross (Mark 15:38). God's most powerful message of love was sent into the place emptied by pain. His messages are still sent there. And if I live to become his and to become like him, I must spend time in that place.

SEEKING SUFFERING

This chapter began with a question about the relevance of the New Testament to the persecution-free church in the modern West. Is the New Testament out of touch, or are we? The intervening paragraphs may elicit an additional question: If suffering is constructive, should I try to suffer? Instead of trying to be good, should I be looking for trouble? The answer to these questions may be found in an appreciation of the forms of suffering described in the New Testament.

Persecution by those who are hostile to the faith is the most obvious form of suffering, the one on which most of the preceding discussion is based. In most cases this understanding underlies general references to suffering. It is a recurrent theme in the teaching of Jesus, and some of his references to persecution have been redefined by later believers to accommodate his teaching to more peaceful circumstances. For example, the Beatitudes promising eternal reward to those who mourn (Matt 5:4) and to the meek (v. 5) were probably understood this way as well as the explicit references to persecution "because of me" (5:10–12). Identification with Jesus, i.e., naming him as supreme authority and acting accordingly, was a threat to the political and religious order of the time. Far-sighted authorities looked beyond the apparent insignificance of the movement to the threat it posed and moved to eliminate it. Jesus was crucified on political charges (Luke 23:2), the first believers were similarly charged (Acts 16:20–21; 17:6–7; 25:7–8), and official persecution continued intermittently throughout the New Testament period (1 Peter 4:14–16; Rev 1:9; 2:9–10). Peter and Paul were martyred according to trustworthy tradition as part of a local purge of Christians in the Roman capital by Nero in the mid-60s. Toward the end of the first century, during the reign of Domitian, heretofore local persecution became empire-wide, and Christianity was officially illegal until the fourth century.

A second form of persecution, which is unofficial and involves more directly the choice of the individual believer, is *social ostracism*. Peter warns that old friends will not take kindly to the believer's renunciation of old practices: "They think it strange that you do not plunge with them into the same flood of dissipation, and they heap abuse on you" (1 Peter 4:4). Paul similarly writes to Timothy that "everyone who wants to live a godly life in Christ Jesus will be persecuted" (2 Tim 3:12). The pain of such exclusion may well be more acute than that of official persecution. It offers no consoling title like "martyr," it is ongoing, and it usually comes from those whose good opinion we would rather have: our colleagues or family members. It requires more willingness than does official persecution—willingness in the face of the powerful inclination to *fit in*.

A third form of suffering is of a still more voluntary nature. The choice *to leave family or possessions* for the sake of dependence on God and service to his kingdom (Mark 10:28–30; Luke 9:57–62; 14:26–33) is suffering in the form of personal insecurity. To surround ourselves with the trappings of comfort, material or social, is natural. It is also natural for them to grow on us, to encrust us, to insulate us, and ultimately to bury us. These harmless little gods work slowly but inexorably, like barnacles on a boat. To attempt to remain aloof while retaining them is a tricky business, as chapter 4 explained: our conduct with these securities indicates our inward attitude toward them. Voluntarily to part with them is the best solution far more often than it is recognized to be. That option is too frightening: What if I change my mind when it is too late to retrieve my securities? Security once lost is not easily rebuilt, and the alternative may be only . . . God. Is he sure enough to warrant that risk? These words are easy enough for me to write, and perhaps not difficult for you to read. The difficulty is in the doing. To deny oneself in order to embrace God is a simple thing—to imagine. It is a painful thing to do.

A fourth form of suffering is not only voluntary but also intensely personal. In both senses it is quite capable of being sought. It is not normally thought of in the context of suffering, and it is doubtful that New Testament authors thought primarily of this when they wrote about constructive pain. But for all these qualifications, *passive virtues* must be included in any discussion of suffering.

The term "passive virtues" refers to the numerous New Testament teachings about nonretaliation in the trying circumstances of everyday life. I will attempt to describe these in more detail in the next chapter, but for now it will suffice to point out that patience, meekness, silence, and forgiveness in the face of opposition and abuse are unnatural to most of us. Because they are so alien, so difficult, so contrary to our inclinations, they may be understood as *actions* even though they appear as nonactions. It causes us pain to act contrary to our natures, and so this self-denial is a form of suffering. It is a dominant theme of the "house-tables"—the New Testament passages that describe the working out of love in social relationships, from family members to the emperor (Eph 5:21–6:9; Col 3:18–4:1; 1 Peter 2:11–3:22). It also takes a prominent place in the enumeration of specific behaviors in several familiar "virtue lists"—the Beatitudes (Matt 5:3–12), the fruit of the Spirit (Gal 5:22–23), and the "love chapter" (1 Cor 13).

A final form of suffering, likewise often unnoticed as such, is *compassion*. In chapter 5 I described it in some detail; the point to stress here is simply that to give compassion is to share pain, to perform a voluntary act of self-denial. No one naturally wants to hurt for another. To do so requires a new nature, a nature like that of Jesus, who had compassion on crowds who were focused not on him but on their own hurts, confusion, and frustration. He knew that they were always ready to turn against him, and eventually they would. But he was always turned *toward them*. In this, even he "learned obedience from what he suffered" (Heb 5:8).

Compassion is the most difficult and therefore the most potent of all forms of suffering. It the least obvious, the most voluntary, the least commendable, the most internal, the least communal, the most draining. For these reasons, it has the most to offer to both the giver and the recipient.

It is not necessary to face martyrdom in order to know the relevance of the New Testament teaching about suffering. Indeed, it is significant that this list of forms of suffering ascends in terms of opportunity as it descends in terms of publicity. The more personally we encounter God's offers to suffer, the more powerfully and the more abundantly he does his work of construction.

Patience:

"Endure All Things"

In the realm of good deeds, nothing is harder to do than nothing. But patience, meekness, silence, and forgiveness in response to offense must be defined largely in terms of activities that are not done. Not to retaliate is usually not to be noticed, much less appreciated. The motivation for such response must be deeper. The reality—the power—that makes patience possible is beneath the surface, where others are unable, and we are afraid, to look. It is natural to prefer the visible, the measurable, the *humanly commendable*. But God resides or does not reside, thrives or does not thrive, in a place of obscurity, out of the public eye. And so it is that in patience he emerges most powerfully. In our invisibility at crucial moments we become windows through which his light shines.

THE PATIENCE OF JESUS

This could almost be expected from a God who bursts on the scene as an illegitimate barn-born peasant, with the bleating of sheep for a trumpet fanfare. This peasant grows up to teach that meek people will inherit the whole earth, that what is inside a person is what really counts, that enemies must be loved, and that it is meaningless to talk about God's forgiveness if one does not forgive others. Finally, he puts all of this into practice throughout a trial on trumped-up charges followed by public mockery, torture, and execution. And all of this, strangely, the peasant does without once saying the words "I am sorry." The absence of that statement from the sayings of Jesus comprises either an enormous contradiction of his otherwise consistent teaching or a powerful confirmation of the central truth of the New Testament: he is not another recipient of forgiveness but the means to forgiveness. In other words, his forgiving is worth infinitely more than the sum total of our forgiving precisely because it is not reciprocal. It flows not from need but from want. God simply, merely, *purely*, wants to give. And as he does so in Jesus, he sets the pattern for a new and radical manner of forgiveness that the New Testament begins to describe.

Of course, it might be argued that Jesus did in fact recognize his own need for forgiveness and that his followers suppressed this in order to exalt him. There are at least two strong but subtle arguments against this. One is that the supposition of a sinless Jesus, one who can forgive but cannot be forgiven, results in a set of implications that were not delved into, and therefore probably not fathomed, by the New Testament writers. More specifically, they did not often draw the connections between incarnation and morality, which we now see as lending depth and coherence to the new faith. The sympathy of Jesus, for example, was not developed as a link between the character of God and the character of a transformed person. We have the advantage of centuries of reflection and comparative literary studies; they moved in a world of blood sacrifice, traditional morals, and recent remarkable events. For them to anticipate the impact of the interconnectedness of these things and then to insert certain data into the text without letting on that they were aware of the implications is improbable in the extreme. They might as well have left behind an unlabeled diagram for an internal combustion engine.

A second argument against the idea that Jesus shares our need for forgiveness is the notion of his self-understanding as it emerges from the sayings that do survive in the Gospels. While he never asserts his own perfection in explicit terms, one cannot read the record of his words and deeds honestly without seeing it "written all over his face," without granting that he sees himself as the focal point of history and the future judge of mankind. To remove this divine (and therefore sinless) aura from Jesus is to remove Jesus from the Gospels, leaving nothing but what we might want to create in our own image. This is a common phenomenon of the last hundred years, from the turn-of-the-century Jesus the Brother of Man to today's Jesus the Existentialist, Socialist, or Therapist. In most of these schemes, the attempt to bring him down to a more "agreeable" level deprives him of any real substance. If we are looking for mere behavioral models, we don't need to travel two millennia to find them. Traveling to find Jesus, however, is a journey toward the substance and the source of patterns. Thus when he forgives, or, more properly, when he accomplishes forgiveness out of his desire rather than his need, he becomes the source for forgiveness. He provides, then, both the *pattern* of patience and forgiveness and the *reason* to be patient and forgiving. As the only one who was pure enough never to need to say "I am sorry," he is now the only one who can purely hear those same words. It is from that vantage point that he asks us to say those words and to hear them from each other.

ENEMIES AND FRIENDS

The preceding chapter considered the centrality of pain in the life of the believer and mentioned the passive virtues, which include patience, meekness, and forgiveness, as possibilities for voluntary and constructive suffering. Part of the task here is to consider these terms, which are so central to the New Testament message, in greater detail. But this is more than an expansion of part of the previous chapter. There is an important shift of focus here from what pain accomplishes for the believer in a hostile world to what pain communicates *about* the believer in a hostile world.

Of course the "hostile world" is difficult to locate. What we encounter are hostile people, people who offend us. The offender may be another believer, and indeed much of the New Testament material on the subject pertains to internal relations in the Christian community. In that sense the instruction fits the preceding part of the book, concerning life within the Christian community, as well as this chapter. But it is useful to consider the subject here because of the breakthrough that the New Testament makes in the categorization of enemies and friends.

The hearers of Jesus understood that their natural enemies were non-Jews, and much of Jesus' time was spent turning this assumption on its head. Your supposed enemies, he said again and again, may be God's friends (Mark 2:15–17), and if they are in need, you have opportunity to be friends to them (Luke 10:29–37). On the other hand, your supposed friends, those you admire, even your own family, may turn out to be true enemies (Mark 3:21, 31–35). If you want to be like God, you must be impartial (Matt 5:43–47) and count as friends those who hunger for God's mercy (Luke 14:12–14). This was more revolutionary than people at that time—especially revolutionaries—wanted to hear. The very idea of loving enemies was novel then. Boundaries between groups and roles within groups were rigidly observed. Outsiders were considered enemies, and insiders were considered friends. There is scarcely any evidence of discomfort with this simplistic distinction, and new attitudes did not follow overnight from new ideas. The idea of including Gentiles in the believing community, for example, was initially difficult to swallow (Acts 10). Later, it was difficult to tolerate the abuse of outsiders such as skeptics, employers, and government officials. Did a middle ground exist between fidelity to the faithful and care for the faithless, between commitment to a "narrow way" and commitment to the demolition of barriers between people? The ground was found in the arena of patience—at times in the literal arena and the bloody ground of persecution.

So it is that while patience begins and remains in the character of God and in the dynamics of Christian community, it must always proceed outward toward a hostile world. Only then does it move full circle as a message of deliverance to its own would-be captors, as a message of life to its own executioners. The gospel lives as its adherents die, and they die little deaths whenever they exercise patience.

THE TERMS OF PATIENCE

Although the ideas behind the terms *patience, meekness,* and *forgiveness* are roughly the same, a brief description of words and their nuances will help to introduce a fuller consideration of the subject.

Patience or endurance is occasionally used in an active sense as persistence in good deeds over time (Mark 13:13; Rom 2:7; Heb 10:36), but it is most often used in its passive sense, a prohibition of retaliation (Rom 12:12; James 5:10; 1 Peter 2:21). Passages that discourage anger (Matt 5:21–22; Eph 4:26; Col 3:8), revenge (Rom 12:19), and verbal retaliation (Mark 14:60–15:5; 1 Cor 4:12; 1 Peter 2:22–23) can be included.

To be meek or gentle is essentially to be nonretributive (Matt 5:5; 2 Cor 10:1; 1 Peter 3:4). The word *meek* carries a connotation of style and so at times serves as a check on a potentially patronizing or judgmental task such as correction (1 Cor 4:21; Gal 6:1; 2 Tim 2:25). Its close relation to patience is evident in this passage:

> My dear brothers, take note of this: Everyone should be quick to listen, slow to speak and slow to become angry, for man's anger does not bring about the righteous life that God desires. Therefore, get rid of all moral filth and the evil that is so prevalent and humbly accept the word planted in you, which can save you (James 1:19–21).

Forgiveness is a more specific term that contains an active element. I do not distinguish that term from those listed above, such as meekness and forgiveness, because it shares with them the fundamental feature that one must make the domain of punishment the domain of God alone. It may also share with the other words the allowance (never the sanction) of wrongdoing and the silent, even anonymous, expression of love. For these reasons it falls into the category that I have chosen to label patience.

THE SUBSTANCE OF FORGIVENESS

What actually happens when one person forgives another? More specifically, does it demand that the person to be forgiven must ask for forgiveness? Does it always involve speaking? If so, what should be said? And if the event of forgiveness is motivated from within, what must happen inside the one forgiving with regard to the wrong: acquittal, compensation, dismissal from memory? We all know the words of forgiveness well enough, but they can be used to manipulate if they do not represent a genuine change of heart.

Consider a typical exchange between a married couple. The man observes the woman's new dress before an evening out and remarks carelessly that it makes her look a bit heavy. She says she is sorry that she doesn't look like a cover girl. He says he is sorry that she is upset, but he just doesn't care for that color on her. She says she is sorry if she overreacted, but she can't handle more personal attacks at the end of a bad day. He says he is sorry that she had a bad day and they might better stay at home. She says that's okay, she will just forget about it and try to have a good time.

Note that in spite of the constant repetition of the words of apology, neither party expresses remorse about anything or releases the other from any obligation. Instead, they exchange low-level attacks from behind the camouflage of some overused expressions. The only clear messages are that she is not sufficiently pretty and that he is not sufficiently kind.

To use the words of forgiveness when there is no intent to apologize or forgive is to cheapen the language to such an extent that the genuine occasion becomes difficult to articulate or even recognize. Like a teenager who learns early to abuse romantic language and sex for self-gratification, the one who abuses forgiveness will have enormous difficulty when "the real thing" comes along. The first principle, then, is to recognize that the occasion for forgiveness is significant, uncommon, and therefore precious.

On the other end of the scale from the glib is the grudge. To extend the analogy just given, if at times we "play the harlot" with the words of forgiveness, at other times we are determined old maids, carefully guarding our resentments against encroachment. We watch most carefully and quietly over the deepest hurts, because their depth consists in their legitimacy, and to voice them is to face them.

Between these extremes is an honest assessment of our own hurt and a quick response to it. Thus Jesus puts relational resolution before religious duty (Matt 5:21–26). Similarly, Paul writes, "In your anger do not sin: Do not let the sun go down while you are still angry, and do not give the devil a foothold" (Eph 4:26–27). The first part of the statement does not constitute approval of anger, which is prohibited elsewhere, including the next paragraph (v. 31;

cf. 2 Cor 12:20; Col 3:8). Rather, Paul is making a concession to the inevitability of anger, while his main point is to resolve such matters as quickly as possible. The New Testament makes it very clear that human anger cannot coexist with patience and forgiveness. This is true for the simple reason that high regard and low regard for another person can alternate, but they cannot occur simultaneously. We try. But our best efforts cannot separate the sin from the sinner either in our imagination or in the sinner's perception, and our own egos are too much involved for our wrath ever to merit the title "righteous indignation."[1] While we "count to ten," it is helpful to remind ourselves that few of the wrongs done to us are deliberate or premeditated or any worse than wrongs we so quickly excuse ourselves for doing. We have much less to forgive than our tempers might indicate.

Perhaps the most detailed account of the activity of forgiveness comes in these commands of Jesus:

> Love your enemies,
> do good to those who hate you,
> bless those who curse you,
> pray for those who mistreat you. (Luke 6:27–28)

This is not a repetitive list. Its constituents provide an important sequence for action. The command to love in the first line is a general heading followed by specifications. The first imperative is simply to do good to the other persons, to find some way to build them up. A verbal response is required by the second specific command to bless. In that culture, a blessing was a formal pronouncement of a desire for

---

[1]Some might attempt to justify wrath by pointing out that Jesus must have felt anger when he turned over the tables of the sellers in the temple (Luke 19:45–46), and on one occasion we are told explicitly that he was angry (Mark 3:4–5). But it is significant that in the latter case Matthew and Luke record the same story but drop the reference to Jesus' anger—obviously to avoid confusion. Jesus' behavior is not considered imitable in these instances; instead, he expresses God's dissatisfaction with sin, and sinners are by definition incapable of sharing his perspective.

God to give good things to someone. The third imperative, to pray for the others, is to ask God to do good things for them. Of course, by this time that prayer has already been answered by one's obedience to the first two commands! At least in part, then, the series is self-fulfilling. It is also significant that these activities can be accomplished, or at least begun, while one still feels hostile toward the other person. But this feeling cannot last. For just as it is impossible simultaneously to love sinners while hating sin, so it is impossible to hate sinners while practicing love. Both love and hate, like the famous hamburger, are "whoppers": two hands are required to hold just one. The metamorphosis of forgiveness is implied even in the sequence of these commands.

Although on the surface it may seem that the easiest item on the list is prayer for one's enemies, since that can be done at a distance, the fact is that it will always be done at a *spiritual* distance until it can be joined to action. The command to act first literally faces us with our hostility and leads us more easily to the place where we can pray sincerely for our enemies. It is all too easy otherwise to convince ourselves never to go beyond prayer, in which case the prayer becomes the self-congratulation of a hypocrite. If the list had to be shortened, then, the first command would have to be the last to go. Actions are the windows of hearts; without them, light can neither emanate nor penetrate. The terminology of forgiveness in the Bible is economic terminology. To be wronged is to have someone in debt to us, and to forgive is to cancel the debt, to forego "collection" (revenge). The clearest example of this is the parable of the unmerciful servant in Matthew 18:23–35, where a message about salvation is conveyed by the story of a financially troubled man whose employer "canceled the debt" (v. 27). Thus it is not surprising to find instruction about forgiveness interwoven with instruction about economic ethics (especially in Luke 6:27–38) or even to find material with dual application

(14:12–14). This terminology may also tell us something about the expectation concerning openness in the "transaction." Release from a financial obligation implies a prior transaction of which both parties are aware; moreover, freedom must be announced to the debtor in order for it to be known. This implies that, in the moral sphere, an apology and a verbalization of forgiveness are appropriate (Luke 17:3–4 makes this more explicit). Verbal exchanges are, however, insufficient and subject to abuse. Just as in the economic sphere, our release of moral debtors can become a form of blackmail. That is why in this section of the chapter I write of the *substance* of forgiveness: words are insufficient and dangerous unless they are accompanied by active love.

We are particularly prone to abuse the substance of forgiveness when we attempt on our own to establish knowledge of the debt in the debtor. At times we even pronounce words of forgiveness in order to procure a confession. The blackmail note begins: "You will apologize for the following, for which I benevolently forgive you. . . ." But, however convinced we are of our own magnanimity, this is manipulative. An extracted apology is a contradiction in terms. A real apology can only be given. The majority of the New Testament passages that tell of the necessity of forgiveness say nothing about apologies, and of course if God had waited for us to apologize before he would act to forgive us, Jesus would never have gotten as far as the cross. But the first words of Jesus from the cross were, "Father, forgive them, for they do not know what they are doing" (Luke 23:34). His love in the face of our defiant lack of remorse is the very thing that coaxes our remorse. Perhaps, then, the best way to understand the role of the apology in the process of forgiveness is that it is the prerequisite, not for love toward the offender, but for complete reconciliation with the offender. "If he listens to you, you have won your brother over" (Matt

18:15). If he does not, the point is that he loses the *enjoyment* of your love, not the fact of it.

THE END OF PATIENCE

In a world of dictators, false prophets, and child molesters, these questions naturally arise: Is there not a legitimate time for endurance to end? Is it not possible for the practice of patience, for radical forgiveness, to serve evil? On the way to inheriting the earth, must one get covered with it?

These are legitimate questions, and the New Testament contains much material about the appropriate range of response to evil. The principle might be put this way: if you choose to make of yourself a doormat, make sure you do it next to a door, not in the middle of the mud. In other words, consider patience not an end but a means to help the offender.

There are a number of models that illustrate this principle and that may find some support in the New Testament. I will consider these in turn from the most to the least active.

There are no examples in the New Testament of violent resistance as a form of response to evil, and there are many texts that explicitly prohibit it (Matt 5:38–42; 26:51–52; Rom 12:17–21). This differs from the Old Testament, where God's people were sometimes called on to exercise his judgment toward others and to establish a nation. Jesus makes it clear that he is not building such an earthly kingdom to be defended (John 18:36).

The early church took a consistently pacifist stance, not (as is popularly supposed) because believers did not like Rome but because they disapproved of killing. This did not change until the fourth century when Christianity became the official religion of the empire and all Christians were required to fight—except, significantly, the clergy. This double standard, which is still with us in the form of military chaplaincy, is entirely out of keeping with the consistent standards for rank-and-file Christians and their leaders within the New Testament. Either all should fight or none should fight. That is an important issue not directly addressed by New Testament writers, for whom it was as yet not relevant. The best that we can do is to look for implications. Certainly one should obey secular authority (Rom 13:1–7), but not when it requires disobedience to God (Acts 5:27–29). And one might choose to turn the other cheek (Matt 5:39) in the context of personal revenge, but does it prevent violence to protect the innocent and punish the guilty on a broader scale? And even if it is wrong to kill, is it not sometimes the lesser of two evils? It may be that in these questions we are faced again with the grace-filled compromise of the seemingly impossible good. A lecturer on the subject impressed me powerfully on just this point. The classic question was posed by someone in the audience: What would this man do if someone burst into his house intending to hurt or kill his wife and son? He replied, "To be honest, I don't know how I would respond. But I know how I would like to respond. I would like to respond just the way God responded to me when I burst into his house and killed his Son."

A second model of resistance in the New Testament is nonviolent but still counteractive. It intends forms of counter-action that are potentially redemptive and therefore constructive. Such direct measures, significantly, are reserved for internal matters. The community governs itself, but it does not exert pressure on those outside. Numerous passages describe the careful exercise of discipline on the part of groups of believers toward individuals who persist in wrongdoing (Matt 18:15–17; 1 Cor 5:9–13; 2 Thess 3:6–15). The principle behind severance from the community, which is the last resort, is that love, not economic or physical force, is the most powerful "weapon" at the disposal of a community of believers. For the community to exclude someone is to deprive that person of its companionship, of its active love. The fact that this should be a community action hints that it is too delicate a matter for frequent occurrence or for individual judgment.

Persuasion is perhaps the most common New Testament form of response "at the end of patience." The forthright proclamation of the injustice of the situation, and the sensitive proposal of a solution, is to interpersonal relations what good preaching is to the salvation of humankind. Paul couples clear instruction with a warning:

> Brothers, if someone is caught in a sin, you who are spiritual should restore him gently. But watch yourself, or you also may be tempted. Carry each other's burdens, and in this way you will fulfill the law of Christ (Gal 6:1–2; cf. 2 Tim 2:24–26).

Silence, seemingly a form of nonresistance, can be a surprisingly loud and penetrating form of response to evil. This is the best form of response to those outside the community of faith, at least in part because it can occur when there is no common ground that would make persuasion or counteraction effective. It is an expression of patience, but to the extent that it communicates tacit disapproval, it can also be a form of response. The supreme example of this is of course Jesus at the time of his trial (cf. 1 Cor 6:7; 1 Peter 3:1–4). Ignatius wrote eighty years later that "the one who truly grasps the word of Jesus is also able to hear his silence, in order that he may be perfect, in order that he may act through his speech and be known through his silence" (Epistle to the Ephesians, 5:2). As both an explicit form of endurance and an implicit form of response, silence expresses the very power that God displays at the pivotal moment in history. At pivotal moments in our histories, yours and mine, just such opportunities will present themselves. Will our endurance, and the end of our endurance, be redemptive?

Boldness:

"Always Be Prepared to Make a Defense"

The Mighty One, God, the LORD,
    speaks and summons the earth
    from the rising of the sun to the place where it sets.
From Zion, perfect in beauty,
    God *shines forth.*
Our God comes and will not be silent;
    a fire devours before him,
    and around him a tempest rages.
                    (Ps 50:1–3, italics mine)

Here is some of the Bible's most beautiful poetry, evoking the image of a God who communicates openly and powerfully to the world. But how does he do that? The key is in the two words *shines forth.*

SHINING AND BOLDNESS

There is a direct link in thought and even vocabulary between the shining of God and the boldness of believers. The progression and connectedness of ideas are impressive.

In the Old Testament, encounters with God were

characterized by bright, blinding light, and this "shining forth" has the double sense of communication or enlightenment concerning God's ways (Deut 33:2; Pss 80:1; 94:1). The light, in a sense, rubs off. Thus Moses, after receiving the law from God on Mount Sinai, shone so brightly himself that he had to wear a veil when he spoke with the people (Exod 34:29–35).

Jesus is the obvious continuation of this theme in the New Testament, and the gospel of John gives it particular emphasis. In the opening paragraph Jesus is described as "the true light that gives light to every man" (John 1:9; cf. Mark 9:1–8). He gives light by declaring the truth about himself in public: "I have spoken *openly* to the world" (John 18:20, italics mine). It is significant that the word "openly" here is a form of the same word translated above as "shines forth."

The noun form of the same word is used numerous times in the New Testament to describe the confidence that believers have before God because of what Jesus accomplished (Eph 3:12; Heb 4:16; 1 John 4:17). This is connected explicitly to Moses by Paul, who explains that the believer no longer needs to fear but may behold the glory of the Lord "with unveiled face" (2 Cor 3:12–18 RSV). Because of this, Paul says, "we are very *bold*" (2 Cor 3:12, italics mine); similarly Luke reports that the apostles "were all filled with the Holy Spirit and spoke the word of God with *boldness*" (Acts 4:31 RSV, italics mine)—again, the same words that lie behind "shines forth." It is no surprise, then, that when all of this comes to the point of a direct command concerning the conduct of believers, Jesus declares, "Let your light *shine* before men" (Matt 5:16, italics mine).

The circle is now complete. The light, or boldness, of the believer flows from a new boldness, or confidence, before God. This flows from the boldness of Jesus in enlightening humankind, which in turn flows from the desire of a perfect

God to shine forth in love. The wonderful and fearful implication is that *we* are the "how" of the psalmist's poem: this God makes *us* into fires, tempests, shining suns. God is bold only as we are bold.

ARE ALL EVANGELISTS?

Boldness involves clear verbal acknowledgment and explanation of God's gift of salvation. But this statement does not in itself reveal the degree of accountability for an individual believer. Does the importance of boldness imply that growth toward perfect obedience will mean becoming a full-time evangelist? If it is acceptable to stop short of that, how short can one stop? The pervasive feeling of guilt in Christian circles concerning evangelism demands fresh and careful consideration of the biblical teaching on the subject.

A survey of the New Testament makes it clear that boldness in the form of verbal evangelism, or "witnessing," as it is popularly called, is not considered a priority for most believers. There is danger in such an observation—more on that later—but a fair reading of the New Testament makes it inevitable.

The overwhelming stress in the New Testament is on action, not speech. The words of Jesus make this clear: "Not everyone who says to me, 'Lord, Lord,' will enter the kingdom of heaven, but only he who does the will of my Father who is in heaven (Matt 7:21; cf. 7:21–27; 24:45–51; 25:31–46; John 14:15–24).

Paul's major epistles say nothing at all about evangelism as a general responsibility, and there are implications to the contrary throughout his writings. In 1 Corinthians 9:16–23 and Ephesians 4:11 he distinguishes evangelists from other believers as having a special function; his instruction to the rank and file in 1 Thessalonians 4:9–10 is that they are to love one another, and, he adds:

> Make it your ambition to lead a quiet life, to mind your own business and to work with your hands, just as we told you, so that your daily life may win the respect of outsiders and so that you will not be dependent on anybody. (1 Thess 4:11–12)

Peter, likewise, instructs believers, "Live such good lives among the pagans that, though they accuse you of doing wrong, they may see your good deeds and glorify God on the day he visits us" (1 Peter 2:12).

But what of the "Great Commission"? Jesus instructed his disciples to "go and make disciples of all nations" (Matt 28:19), and his parting words were "You will be my witnesses in Jerusalem, and in all Judea and Samaria, and to the ends of the earth" (Acts 1:8). Are not all believers his disciples, and do not all therefore share equally the responsibility to *tell* the good news? The record appears to indicate otherwise. In the first chapters of Acts, only Peter preached. Later the names of John, Stephen, and Philip are added. Still later Paul became the focus. In two places (Acts 4:31 and 8:4) it is apparent that an unknown number of others who were not apostles were acting as evangelists, but the vagueness of these passages, coupled with the absence of instruction about evangelism for believers in general elsewhere in the New Testament, suggests that these few passages should not be regarded as implied instructions for all. A strong hint in this direction is supplied by the listing of "evangelists" in Ephesians 4:11-12 among those given gifts that God supplies "so that the body of Christ may be built up." While all believers share responsibilities for conduct (e.g., joy, unity, patience), not all have the same functions in the advancement of the gospel (1 Cor 12:1–31). Most of the functions that are listed involve work within the community (Rom 12:6–8; 1 Cor 12:8–10; Eph 4:11). Certain people, including the Twelve but not limited to them, have a particular function to communicate the faith to those outside. And this is the key point in terms of application: these people were not necessarily the most obedient, but they were peculiarly suited and prepared by God for this important work. Not everyone is.

BOLDNESS AND THE EVANGELISTIC FUNCTION

Before considering the relevance of boldness to other believers, it will be useful to describe briefly the substance and style of the work of these specialists. To the extent that their responsibility represents only a difference in quantity, it is useful to examine the quality of their work.

The content or essence of the message, technically termed the *kerygma*, is repeated in various forms throughout the New Testament, and it is particularly clear in the very first sermon of Peter in Acts 2: Jesus fulfills the hope of the Jews as the Scriptures describe it (vv. 14–22); he died as part of God's plan (v. 23); he was raised and exalted to heaven (vv. 24–36); and all must therefore repent, believe, and be baptized (vv. 37–41).

For Peter, Paul, and undoubtedly others in the New Testament period whose names are not so prominent, delivery of this message was a full-time activity, and it had almost exclusive priority. They preached and moved on, following a pattern laid down by Jesus himself (Mark 1:14–15), who occasionally sent his own disciples out on short missionary trips (Mark 6:7–13). Paul rarely stayed in one location longer than a few weeks, and even in those places where he invested more time he referred to himself as a mere planter (1 Cor 3:6).

What is amazing is the nature of that planting on the part of these few, and indeed since then of all others who, armed only with the power of the truth, have conquered new territories. So the political-religious establishment of the then strong and confident Jewish nation was astounded "when they saw the courage of Peter and John, and realized that they were unschooled, ordinary men" (Acts 4:13). "We must obey God rather than men!" (Acts 5:29), says Peter to the death-wielding authorities. This is the same man who one night only weeks before was cringing in fear before female servants who suspected him of knowing Jesus (Matt 26:69–72). Paul, likewise, stood fearless before such varied potential intimidators as the intellectual elite of Athens (Acts 17:22–31), the rioters of Ephesus (Acts 19:30), and the Roman ruler of the Jews (Acts 26:24–29). Paul's boldness took a comedic turn in this last account when the procurator accused Paul of going beyond self-defense to evangelism, and Paul replied, "I pray God that not only you but all who are listening to me today may become what I am, except for these chains" (Acts 26:29). From here his courage took him to Rome where his example would embolden others (Phil 1:12–14). There the narrative leaves him waiting to take his case to the emperor himself (Acts 25:11–12),[1] and although we have no reliable information beyond this point, Paul's track record leaves little doubt that not even Lord Caesar could intimidate someone who served an infinitely greater Lord. It is clear that the source of Paul's boldness was his intimacy with God, not his own abilities or status (1 Cor 2:3–5; 2 Cor 5:11–15).

The person who assumes the function of people like Peter and Paul in the modern world should not do so hastily. Although the process is not described in detail, it is clear at least that the function of an evangelist in the New Testament era involved the consensus of the community. This in turn implies that the person had to be mature and knowledgeable. The need for care has hardly diminished with the passing of centuries. There is some legitimacy to the modern complaint

---

[1]Paul appealed his case to Caesar not because he wanted to escape punishment at the hands of lower officials, but because he wanted to argue for imperial rather than mere local or regional recognition of the new religion. He was wise enough to recognize that his own education and background qualified him uniquely to do this.

against youthful enthusiasts who approach strangers with a slogan-ridden message of salvation. This is not the boldness to which the New Testament refers; it is more commonly the rudeness which the New Testament prohibits. All too often it is motivated by a sense of obligation to speak rather than by passionate concern for those who hear. Occasionally the quick, intrusive approach bears fruit, and so more are encouraged to try it: no one returns to report on the number of people who were further hardened in their opposition to the truth by the insensitivity of its messengers. The real tragedy is that these novices are doing what those better qualified should be doing, especially when in their zeal the novices move beyond those within their own circle of knowledge and life experience.

BOLDNESS AND THE BELIEVER

What then is the responsibility of the believer who is not an evangelist in the technical sense? There are several New Testament texts that make the general expectation clear. The most often quoted of these texts is the command in 1 Peter 3:15: "Always be prepared to give an answer to everyone who asks you to give the reason for the hope that you have." Even here the message is not divorced from the method: Peter continues, "But do this with gentleness and respect, keeping a clear conscience, so that those who speak maliciously against your good behavior in Christ may be ashamed of their slander" (v. 16). Paul gives similar advice in Colossians 4:5–6: "Be wise in the way you act toward outsiders; make the most of every opportunity. Let your conversation be always full of grace, seasoned with salt, so that you may know how to answer everyone."

The implication of these passages is that one should be ready when called upon to answer for oneself and indeed to be the kind of person whose words and deeds will arouse positive curiosity. This hardly constitutes a command to be an evangelist as we commonly define the work, but neither does it constitute an excuse for silence as a cover for shallowness or embarrassment. The continual readiness described here requires breadth and depth of preparation, imagination and sensitivity in expression, and, above all, an eye ever looking for opportunities. This is not a life for those who are weak and timid within. It is a life for those whose boldness before a bold God enables them to look with new eyes at the world.

In this regard the rank and file play an important part between the evangelist and the outsider. In the family or in the workplace, they present the evidence of a new order of life. When asked, they are ready to begin an explanation of this. But they are also members of a community, and the existence of this community is a more powerful message than any of its parts, or even the sum of its parts. Individuals must bring outsiders in to see this and to hear an explanation of the phenomenon. This sensible sequence is thrown off when either mass evangelism or individual evangelism are separated from the everyday life of the one who communicates and from the community of believers. It may be safer to the ego to hide behind a television screen or a one-time encounter, but in the long run everyone involved loses. Genuine boldness not only begins at home, but it can afford to stay there.

· 12 ·

Self-Control:

"Flee Immorality"

Striving toward the goal of goodness like a runner straining to reach the finish line is familiar imagery in the New Testament. The focus should be on the "prize" (Phil 3:13–14) or the "crown" (2 Tim 4:7–8) and on Jesus, who ran before and ran perfectly (Heb 12:1–2). But this race is not a prance around a clean oval track. The path winds uphill through rough terrain, and at times there is a sense that something hostile is sneaking behind or lurking beside on the path. At such moments the destination is less certain than the danger, and the journey seems less of a race than a chase. As Peter warns, "Your enemy the devil prowls around like a roaring lion looking for someone to devour" (1 Peter 5:8). "Be self-controlled," he writes, "and alert." *There is something back there.*

For us, the image of dangerous wild animals is unfamiliar. What most of us have experienced, however, is the step-quickening fear that occurs when we find ourselves isolated at night in a crime-ridden city. Any figure glimpsed in the shadows, any noise behind us, is a potential danger. What should we expect to see if we look around in the dark? Not the devil, certainly. If he or his troops are back there tracking us, they are not stupid enough to show themselves, knowing that such direct evidence of supernatural forces at work would only speed us up. No, what we are more likely to see are the familiar objects that pursue us, beckoning, all day long—objects that cause us no fear in the easy daylight. A provocative mannequin in a storefront, a come-hither face on a billboard, a neon-framed vixen in a liquor store window poster. Just inanimate faces in the dark, nothing to be afraid of. Or perhaps we see only a dark piece of glass reflecting in the streetlamp light our own form and we pause to make sure. The face is blank—why waste expression on a mirror?—and we move on, perhaps feeling a bit more lonely than alone. There was nothing to merit that quickened pulse, there was nothing there pursuing in the dark, right?

Wrong. And perhaps it is only in the dark and quiet of a city street at night that we can see clearly the barrage that meets each of us in our loneliness and creates an overwhelming pressure to stop running, to relax, to indulge ourselves. To resist this pressure is to know what the New Testament writers call "self-control."

SELF-CONTROL OF WHAT?

"Self-control" is often construed as a general term for the capacity to accomplish anything in an ordered or disciplined manner, from Bible reading to weight reduction. With respect to abstinence, the word is applied to everything from alcohol to wrath. But these categories are too broad to be meaningful, and they do not reflect biblical usage. In the New Testament, self-control has a specific focus. It refers to the subjugation of sensual appetites, especially the appetites for food, drink, or sex. Its opposite is license or excess in the same areas, and for these a variety of terms are used. The opposition of sensual desires to self-controlled living is most clear in Galatians

5:21–23, where drunkenness and orgies (involving food as well as sex) end Paul's list of behaviors to avoid, while self-control ends his list of "Spirit fruit" behaviors.

The abuses of food and alcohol or other substances take somewhat different forms in our culture than in the world of the New Testament. Increased affluence, leisure, and personal freedom have made the abuse of food and addictive substances possible for more people, and the resulting rampant social problems merit the great amount of attention given to them. In the New Testament, little attention is paid to these problems apart from occasional prohibitions of excess (e.g., Luke 21:34; Rom 13:13; 1 Peter 4:3). The principles are clear and still relevant, however difficult they may be to apply. Excess leads to addiction, which leads to destruction. The responsible person, therefore, will excercise control prior to the point of excess. There are better things to do with your time, Paul argues, than to get drunk. "For the kingdom of God is not a matter of eating and drinking, but of righteousness, peace and joy in the Holy Spirit" (Rom 14:17; cf. Eph 5:15–20).

Eating disorders and substance abuse are contemporary problems related to self-control, and they demand careful consideration, but the constraints of space require that I make a choice about the focus of this chapter, and that focus will be on sexuality. This choice reflects the great amount of attention given to sexuality in the New Testament and the greater number of people concerned. There also appears to exist an even greater amount of ambiguity with regard to sex. The relevant New Testament passages, even when they are clear, do not answer all of the questions raised in our modern context, and those that are clear may be clouded by the fog of diverse interpretations or the smoke of our own passions. It is pointless to advocate fleeing from immorality if we do not know what it is either to be immoral or to flee.

But even to begin a consideration of requirements is

objectionable in one sense. Jesus did not come to give a new purity code but to set people free. Thus to define self-control in negative terms, to define sexuality only by describing what people should *not* do, is to misconstrue the intent of the New Testament and to realize at the end of this book the worst fears of many who began it. But it is not necessary to proceed in such a fashion. To be sure, it is essential at some points to define limits, but even then the stress should be on the good reasons for the restriction, and it should flow from a positive model. Self-control, properly understood, is not a system of abstinence from all but one arbitrary option. It is, rather, one ingredient in the creation of a beautiful object—lifelong monogamy.

WHY MONOGAMY?

The New Testament instructions about sexuality rest on a very old foundation. The first chapter of Genesis affirms God's satisfaction with creation. As each day of creation ends, he sees that it is good. And after man is created in God's image, "male and female," and told to "be fruitful and increase in number," God sees that it is *very* good (Gen 1:27–31). When the creation of humankind is expanded in the second chapter, the woman is created as a "suitable helper," with the result that from then on "a man will leave his father and mother and be united to his wife, and they will become one flesh" (Gen 2:20–24). Thus—appropriately enough, in poetic form—the essence of the positive biblical model of sexual union is communicated. Perhaps we would not appreciate the affirmations included in this story if we humans did not have a history—especially in recent times—of denying them. But there are at least four crucial affirmations in this account that generate most New Testament commands and prohibitions.

The first affirmation is the goodness of sexual differentiaion, the truth that we are two sexes in fellowship: "male and female he created them." The second is that the physical union of male and female is intended to produce children: "be fruitful and increase in number." The third is that the sexes complement each other socially, in that the woman is created for companionship: she is a "suitable helper." The fourth affirmation is threefold: implicit in the act of "leaving and cleaving" to become "one flesh" are the notions of equality, exclusivity, and permanence.

Deviations from these affirmations came later. Repressive male chauvinism came almost immediately, not long after Adam blamed his own fall on "the woman you put here with me" (Gen. 3:12). So much for companionship, the third affirmation. From that point onward, woman was in subjugation to man (Gen 3:16), and she quickly devolved to the status of *property* in the Jewish legal system. The multifold fourth affirmation was denied soon afterward in the forms of polygamy, divorce, prostitution, and adultery. Later, Jesus spoke of internal betrayal in the form of lust. More recently, we have raised to epidemic proportions two other deviations rarely mentioned in biblical times: premarital intercourse and rape. The first and second affirmations of the Genesis narrative are not exempt from violation either. They are negated by any practical rejection of heterosexuality: bestiality, denial of gender distinctions, homosexuality, abortion, and even some forms of celibacy.

"Where there is a will, there is a way," the saying goes. In the garden, there was but one will and one good way. Afterwards, outside the garden, other wills have produced a myriad of ways. Have we improved on the garden by building Hollywood Boulevard?

A FEW STEPS FURTHER

It may be possible to extend the affirmations of the Genesis account by applying New Testament principles and reflecting on common experience to build a stronger case for monogamy. My hope is that the following attempt can be refined and deepened by the cooperative efforts of sociologists, psychologists, and theologians.

Only heterosexual union has the potential to produce offspring. The strongest bond takes place between mother, father, and child when all three know that the father is indeed the father of that particular child and when both parents are acting responsibly as caregivers for each other and for the child. As the loving union of the parents continues, the child is able to observe positive models of sexual differentiation and division of labor. In other words, the growing child is able to learn about unity and diversity, about community, and about cooperation. Healthy love in a nuclear family is difficult to accomplish. It may be that nothing is more difficult, because nothing is more intimate and therefore more threatening. But in terms of the values and behaviors expressed in earlier chapters, nothing could be more valuable than to grow up in the midst of a healthy marriage. To be immersed in it is to learn to swim in the waters of the wider family of believers. All of the principles of loyalty, consideration, cooperation, openness, affection, and respect are bred in a healthy family. Thus nothing can serve the family of Father, Son, and Holy Spirit better than the family of father, mother, and child. It is not only for its own sake, then, that this bond should be strong and permanent. The relation of husband to wife is exalted to the point where it is compared to the relation of the risen Jesus to the body of believers, which is an eternal and ever-growing union of mutual service and affection (Eph 5:25–33).

The analogy is intimidating to the most successful marriage partners, to say nothing of those who have known frustration and failure in attempting to build a lasting relationship. But at least in some respects it is attainable. And certainly as a point of comparison to the supreme relationship—that between Christ and the church—marriage must be considered the supreme opportunity to practice the love that Christ himself models and gives.

What we must come to grips with is the fact that while we are pursuing this love, we are also being pursued—by powerful forces at work in our world, forces that play on various competing desires within ourselves. The New Testament, assuming the positive model outlined above, addresses most of these deviations as opportunities for self-control. Any organizational scheme is somewhat arbitrary, but I will follow the outline provided by the affirmations of Genesis in addressing, successively, behaviors that deny sexual differentiation, behaviors that deny procreation, and behaviors that deny permanence.

HOMOSEXUALITY

The single clear statement in the New Testament concerning homosexuality is Romans 1:27–28, where Paul, speaking of the outcome of idol worship on the part of Gentiles, explains that

> because of this, God gave them over to shameful lusts. Even their women exchanged natural relations for unnatural ones. In the same way the men also abandoned natural relations with women and were inflamed with lust for one another. Men committed indecent acts with other men, and received in themselves the due penalty for their perversion.

Paul speaks of "natural" in this context as a reference to biological functions, not to "inclinations," as the word is used by some today. An argument rages between those who think that homosexual inclination is biologically determined and those who think that it is environmentally determined, but the debate is irrelevant to Paul's argument. Whatever the source of the inclination, it is a departure from the obvious reproductive function of heterosexual intercourse. It is not possible to refute this by claiming that heterosexual foreplay or nonreproductive intercourse are also departures, because these activities are part of a potentially reproductive whole.

The argument from biological "naturalness" also refutes the claim that Paul was prohibiting only pederasty (sex between men and boys), which was the prevalent form of homosexual behavior in the Gentile world at the time of Paul's writing. The terms used here and elsewhere that have been understood traditionally to condemn homosexual practice (1 Cor 6:9; 1 Tim 1:10; 2 Peter 2:6–7; Jude 7) do not spell out the behavior precisely, but this is hardly necessary. Whether the authors had in mind men with boys, men with their own male slaves, men with male prostitutes, or consenting adults, they knew that none of these combinations would produce families.

The prohibition of homosexual activity goes back to the holiness code in Leviticus, which describes homosexual activity as "detestable" and deserving of death (Lev 18:22; 20:13). This is grounded in the principle of purity, an affirmation of order that demands that different "kinds" of things not be mixed or confused. To deny one's sexual differentiation in a homosexual relationship constitutes denial of this principle. There is ample evidence that Jews during the New Testament period and post–New Testament Christians followed this principle and consistently regarded homosexual activity as sin. To argue that Jesus threw out this principle along with ceremonial laws regarding pure and impure foods and that his followers were too "homophobic" to apply his liberating principles is wrong for at least two reasons. First, the holiness code in the surrounding verses of Leviticus 18 and 20 uses the same terminology of purity in condemning incest and bestiality—behaviors that the homosexual would hardly defend. Secondly, to extrapolate from freedom in eating certain foods to freedom in copulating is to ignore the relation of homosexual activity to reproduction and hence to human wholeness. Consumption of food does not produce children.

Having said all of this, it must also be said that the attitude of repulsion directed toward the homosexual minority on the part of the heterosexual majority is insensitive and hypocritical in the extreme. Homosexual activity is impure, but it is no *more* impure than adultery or other heterosexual deviations from the biblical norm. Why is the person who is angered by the sight of a gay couple walking arm-in-arm not equally repulsed by the more common sight on television or in films of adulterous or unwed couples writhing hip-to-hip? Or more to the point, why is that person not equally repulsed by his or her own heterosexual lusts? If anything, the homosexual deserves much more sympathy, because self-control for the homosexual does not allow for the physical release in marriage that can help the heterosexual who has an inclination for adultery. In order to strive for conformity to the biblical model, the homosexual must change in orientation or at least practice celibacy—a much greater challenge than to wait for a mate or to limit oneself to a single mate. Homosexuals, especially those suffering from AIDS, are the modern equivalents of lepers, and we may be increasing the problem by encouraging their isolation in colonies. Without a doubt, if Jesus came in the twentieth century as he did in the first, he would cause a scandal by associating with homosexuals—not in order to display his own inclinations, but to offer the transforming power of his love. The principle, and the challenge, are the same: Can anyone who has been touched by Jesus' compassion refuse to extend that touch to the outcasts of the world?

ABORTION AND REFUSAL TO PROCREATE

The New Testament says nothing about abortion, and there is no clear teaching on the subject in the Old

Testament. The Jews and the early Christians were, however, clear and unanimous in their condemnation of the practice, which was common in the Roman world. They called it murder, because the product of sexual union, however unplanned or unwanted, would in most cases become a human being who would eventually be happy not to have been aborted. In a tiny minority of cases today—those involving rape, incest, or severe health risks to mother or child—there is cause for debate. But what is euphemistically called "pro-choice" today is in the vast majority of cases an after-the-fact refusal to face the consequences of *poor* choice— the choice to have sex purely for pleasure.

"But what about all of those unwanted children?" the reporters once asked Mother Theresa. "Give them to me," she replied, "I want them." I do believe that she was quite serious. What I hear in her statement is the voice of Christ, speaking again as he spoke through other "fools" in the Roman Empire who gave us history's first orphanages and hospices in response to very similar social problems. We can do the same today—if we spend more time loving the unloved than we spend hating certain politicians and physicians.

Consideration of abortion should not be divorced from consideration of other negations of reproduction. Celibacy that places a higher priority on service to the kingdom than on the responsibilities of a family can be commendable, as the example of Jesus and the instruction of Paul affirm (1 Cor 7:1–9; 25–38). Paul is careful to qualify his recommendation by affirming marriage and even by granting that strong sexual desire is ample ground to disregard his recommendation. He commends one who is celibate while waiting for marriage, after a spouse's death, or temporarily by mutual consent within a marriage for the purpose of spiritual focus. These forms of celibacy supplant the positive model of sexuality without denying it. In all of these models, procreation is a good that yields in these various circumstances to a greater good.

There are, however, two forms of celibacy that constitute practical denials of procreation and thus approximate abortion. Both of these forms developed after the New Testament was written. The first was borrowed from the pagan philosophical notion that matter, and therefore sex, was evil. Asceticism and a long history of sexual inhibition within marriage has been the result. This is contrary to the biblical material, which includes the Old Testament Song of Songs, a warm and open tribute to erotic love in marriage. Some interpreters view it as an allegory about Christ, but the sensible reader will still give it an "R" rating at face value and recognize its celebration of healthy sexual expression.

Another form of celibacy is entirely modern and is dependent entirely on the advent of effective methods of birth control. I refer to the decision to have sex but not to have children. It might be argued that any use of birth control—even abstention for one night—is a form of celibacy. But the decision not to be a parent at all is qualitatively different from the decision to limit the size of a family or the decision to control the timing of childbearing. It assumes, on the basis of a recently developed luxury, that the pleasure of sex is an end in itself. Such an assumption is careless. It certainly contributes to the epidemic of abortion and unwanted children when birth control fails. But more importantly, the limitation of sex to pleasure represents a refusal to take the gift of oneself (of which sex is just one expression) to another level, to the level of giving one's united self—male and female—to a new life. In other words, there is a progression in family living and a responsibility to grow in giving as one matures. Imagine a child saying, "I like being eleven, and since there is now a drug available to keep me eleven until I die, I think I'll just stay here in my room and play video games until then. The idea of junior high school scares me. Call me when supper is ready."

DIVORCE

Jesus prohibits divorce and refers to remarriage after divorce as adultery (Mark 10:1–12; Luke 16:18; cf. 1 Cor 7:10–16). The principle behind his prohibition of remarriage is the permanent unity of the marriage bond. No human authority, neither the consent of the parties involved nor a legal proceeding, can break a union established by God: "They are no longer two, but one. Therefore what God has joined together, let man not separate" (Mark 10:9). To remarry, then, is to ignore the permanent bond and amounts to adultery.

This explanation appears to be contradicted by the two parallel passages in Matthew that seem to contain an exception to the prohibition: "Everyone who divorces his wife except on the ground of *porneia* makes her an adulteress" (Matt 5:32; cf. 19:9). I have left untranslated the key word, which is usually translated "unchastity" or "unfaithfulness." It is unlikely that *porneia* means adultery, or at least not *only* adultery, since a more specific word could have been used. If the word has a broader definition, it is still strictly sexual and physical. *Porneia* may refer to incest, as in cases where a Gentile couple would enter the believing community and be found to have been married in violation of the more strict Jewish incest laws. In such a case the marriage was discontinued. Another possibility is that the traditional examination of the bride on her wedding day would produce evidence that she was "unchaste," i.e., not a virgin. To modern readers, this would look like a broken engagement, not a divorce. But in ancient times marriage began with betrothal, not the wedding ceremony, and so a broken betrothal was a divorce (so Joseph intended to "divorce"

Mary [Matt 1:19]). Still another possibility is that the text is not giving an exception at all but is simply defining terms. In other words, a divorce for the reason of *porneia*, while still wrong, cannot technically produce adultery, because the unfaithfulness has already taken place.

While I favor this last interpretation, it is clear that none of the possibilities allow for the broad modern definitions of *porneia* which justify divorce on almost any ground. Nor is there allowance of remarriage in any of these passages. Even in the "exception" account in Matthew, the exception applies to divorce, not to remarriage. Luke's version could not be more plain: "Anyone who divorces his wife and marries another woman commits adultery, and the man who marries a divorced woman commits adultery" (Luke 16:18). To lend biblical sanction to one more divorce or remarriage on the basis of a debatable reading of the one clause in the entire Bible that is open to dispute is the supreme example of self-serving interpretation.

ADULTERY, PROSTITUTION, AND LUST

The New Testament is no less stringent in its statements about adultery. In Jewish law, adultery had to do with property. In order to insure inheritance and the preservation of the family structure, it was important to be sure who was the father of a child. Thus *any* sexual activity outside marriage was taboo for women, but for men only sex with married women was severely punished. But the New Testament goes beyond property laws and family structure to ground instructions in the permanence of the marriage bond and in the intent of the heart. Paul, for example, argues that a believer "who unites himself with a prostitute is one with her in body," but that same believer is "a temple of the Holy Spirit," and "one with him in spirit" (1 Cor 6:12–20). In other words, to join with any other outside the marriage bond is not only to violate the permanence and exclusivity of that bond but also to involve the Lord himself in the sin. Recalling the scene of the opening chapter, when the door swings open and we are exposed in our wrongdoing, engagement in extramarital sex is like saying, "Come, join us in the bed, Lord." It is a horrible thought, but it is one worth considering if we are to take our bodies seriously—as God does.

Jesus took all of this a step further by extending inward the purity of the marriage bond: "Anyone who looks at a woman lustfully has already committed adultery with her in his heart" (Matt 5:28). It is no secret that "from within, out of men's hearts, come evil thoughts, sexual immorality, . . . " (Mark 7:21). Infidelity in its many forms grows not out of external pressure but out of an active fantasy life. Fantasies get old and stale if they are not enlivened by new and exciting material in the form of visual experiences. Visual experiences and masturbation are not quite as exciting as physical contact with a member of the opposite sex. And so, inexorably, a person can feel self-controlled by walking ever closer to the line without stepping over until one day the line is not noticed. Which drink makes one an alcoholic? Which meal makes one a glutton? Self-control begins far behind the line and within the person, in the mental world visible only to that person and One other.

SEX BEFORE MARRIAGE

The implications of the exclusive marriage bond for the question of premarital sex may be obvious. The New Testament makes no explicit statements, but that is due to the rarity, not the permission, of premarital sex. Philo of Alexandria, a Jewish contemporary of Jesus, plainly states the Jewish position, which was adopted by Christians: "Before the legal union we do not have sex with other women, but come as virgin men to virgin maidens."[1] The principle is the same as that which applies to adultery—the multiplication of a bond that is meant to be exclusive.

Porneia, often translated "fornication" and applied in our day to premarital sex, was probably understood in the New Testament context to apply primarily to sex with prostitutes. But it is a general word, and in principle it applies to sex before marriage. The most obvious example of this is 1 Thessalonians 4:3–6:

> It is God's will that you should be sanctified: that you should avoid sexual immorality [*porneia*]; that each of you should learn to control his own body in a way that is holy and honorable, not in passionate lust like the heathen, who do not know God; and that in this matter no one should wrong his brother or take advantage of him.

The principle here is consideration of the other person. It is directed primarily to the male, suggesting that he has an obligation not only to keep his own sexual activity within marriage, but also to contribute to the health of other marriages by not having sex with the potential partners of other men.

There are good reasons for self-control that apply particularly to premarital sex, especially in our own day. Unmarried people face a great deal of frustration, both because our culture—particularly the music and visual media—creates overwhelming pressure toward promiscuity, and because most young adults face a long period of waiting between the time they reach sexual maturity and the time they are marriageable. The dating ritual compounds the difficulty by creating a pattern of conquest rather than practice in meaningful relationships. Especially for those who are active and attractive, an understanding develops that romance and sex are important as adventures rather than as

---

[1]*On Joseph* 6:43.

celebrations of lifelong commitment. The attitude inevitably spills over into marriage: sex becomes boring soon after the honeymoon, and the spouse merely provides data for an already established fantasy life. Mental betrayal easily becomes physical betrayal. "Oh, but I can control it after I'm married," you respond. Good for you, if you can break out of the trap and experience happy monogamy. But what about the partners of your past? Are they all so able, or have you helped them down a road that will end in broken hearts and broken marriages? Or even if your sexual activity stopped short of intercourse, did that fact make it easier for your partners to exercise control in subsequent relationships? Those people still exist somewhere, even if you have forgotten their names. You may not know the disease, but you may be carrying it to others.

BUILDING A CONTROL SYSTEM

This is a frustrating subject even for those who have exercised control. Many women are forced to say no for so long that they develop inhibitions and cannot help but consider even married sex as somehow "dirty." Many men attempt to draw a line at fantasy and masturbation, but they find later that no woman, including their wife, can measure up to "sweet imagination." Is there any practical help to be had?

The New Testament makes a strong case for dissociation from the world (2 Cor 6:14–18; 1 John 2:15–17), not in the sense of isolation from people but in the sense of isolation from corrupting influences (1 Cor 5:9–10). This will mean different things in different situations, but some specifics will clarify the principle of dissociation. Breaking off destructive relationships is one example (1 Peter 4:3–4). Another example is modesty in dress (3:3-4)—particularly relevant to women who are often (at least consciously) unaware of the force of visual stimulation for most men.

The obvious implication of this for men is to avoid, as much as possible, scenes that feed the imagination: nightclub dances, beaches, television and films, fashion magazines, and popular music. There is nothing legally pornographic about any of this. But porn is as porn does, and the fact is that we live in a world that sends a message of indulgence in far more subtle forms than those found in "adult" bookstores. "If anyone regards something as unclean, then for him it is unclean" (Rom 14:14). If it serves the function of an erotic stimulus, this axiom applies even to the Sears catalog lingerie section. The person who is serious about self-control will find useful a very broad definition of what is dangerous.

Much of the New Testament's instruction and my own remarks appear to display a male bias, especially when the stress is on visual stimuli as a barrier to self-control. But even after discounting, the stress is worth considering, especially in our own day. The image of the "ideal" woman is employed in our culture to sell products to both men and women. The message is clear: men must buy products to attract such women, and women must buy products to look like such women and so to attract men. Because men generally take the initiative in making potential romantic contacts, women feel compelled to attract attention visually. Once in a relationship, any insecurity on the part of the woman is likely to be exploited in light of the "ideal" image and used to gain sexual gratification. It is a buyer's market—and one in which the value of women as persons has been reduced to an all-time low by the sexual revolution. The problem of self-control for women, then, may be largely derivative of the problem for men. And however we may analyze the problem, the result is clearly destructive for both sexes.

There is definitely something lurking back there behind you as you walk in the night. When you turn around, if you see it, you see that it smiles, it waves, it flirts. Call it the world, or the flesh, or the devil, but recognize what it wants. It wants to find a way—any way—to keep you from going forward. It knows that the way forward, the way of self-control, is the way back to the garden.

• Conclusion •

Getting There From Here

To love God, practice humility, rejoice in the Lord, pray without ceasing, and renounce possessions. To love other believers, practice sympathy, be of the same mind, submit to one another, and build one another up verbally. To live lovingly in the world, recognize the importance of suffering, exercise patience, boldly represent your beliefs, and control your inclination for sensual indulgence.

These are good things to strive for, good things to think about seriously and often. The life of striving involves not only deciding between good and bad but also deciding between *goods*. This ability to discern is crucial, and it demands immersion in God's presence through prayer, time invested in other people, and serious study. Paul summarized one of his letters this way:

> Finally, brothers, whatever is true,
> whatever is noble, whatever is right,
> whatever is pure, whatever is lovely,
> whatever is admirable—if anything is
> excellent or praiseworthy—think about
> such things. (Phil 4:8)

The good things listed in the first paragraph correspond to the subjects of each part and each chapter of this book. We are attracted to them. But attraction is not action. Somehow, having believed and having understood some of the implications of that belief, we want strength to do what we know to be good. And so this last chapter must be more than a summary. It must be more personal. It must be about power.

MABEL

I was a college student when I met Mabel. It was Mother's Day, and I was taking some flowers to the county convalescent home to brighten the day for some lonely mothers and grandmothers.

This state-run convalescent hospital is not a pleasant place. It is large, understaffed, and overfilled with senile and helpless and lonely people who are waiting to die. On the brightest of days it seems dark inside, and it smells of sickness and stale urine. I went there once or twice a week for four years, but I never wanted to go there, and I always left with a sense of relief. It is not the kind of place one gets used to.

On this particular day I was walking in a hallway that I had not visited before, looking in vain for a few who were alive enough to receive a flower and a few words of encouragement. This hallway seemed to contain some of the worst cases, strapped onto carts or into wheelchairs and looking completely helpless.

As I neared the end of this hallway, I saw an old woman strapped up in a wheelchair. Her face was an absolute horror. The empty stare and white pupils of her eyes told me that she was blind. The large hearing aid over one ear told me that she was almost deaf. One side of her face was being eaten by cancer. There was a discolored and running sore covering part of one cheek, and it had pushed her nose to one side, dropped one eye, and distorted her jaw so that what should have been the corner of her mouth was the bottom of her mouth. As a consequence, she drooled constantly. I was told later that when new nurses arrived, the supervisors would send them to feed this woman, thinking that if they could stand this sight they could stand anything in the building. I also learned later that this woman was eighty-nine years old and that she had been here, bedridden, blind, nearly deaf, and alone, for twenty-five years. This was Mabel.

I don't know why I spoke to her—she looked less likely to respond than most of the people I saw in that hallway. But I put a flower in her hand and said, "Here is a flower for you. Happy Mother's Day." She held the flower up to her face and tried to smell it, and then she spoke. And much to my surprise, her words, although somewhat garbled because of her deformity, were obviously produced by a clear mind. She said, "Thank you. It's lovely. But can I give it to someone else? I can't see it, you know, I'm blind."

I said, "Of course," and I pushed her in her chair back down the hallway to a place where I thought I could find some alert patients. I found one, and I stopped the chair. Mabel held out the flower and said, "Here, this is from Jesus."

That was when it began to dawn on me that this was not an ordinary human being. Later I wheeled her back to her room and learned more about her and her history. She had grown up on a small farm that she managed with only her mother until her mother died. Then she ran the farm alone until 1950 when her blindness and sickness sent her to the convalescent hospital. For twenty-five years she got weaker and sicker, with constant headaches, backaches, and stomach aches, and then the cancer came too. Her three roommates were all human vegetables who screamed occasionally but never talked. They often soiled their bedclothes, and because the hospital was understaffed, especially on Sundays when I usually visited, the stench was often overpowering.

Mabel and I became friends over the next few weeks, and I went to see her once or twice a week for the next three years. Her first words to me were usually an offer of hard candy from a tissue box near her bed. Some days I would read to her from the Bible, and often when I would pause she would continue reciting the passage from memory, word-for-word. On other days I would take a book of hymns and sing with her, and she would know all the words of the old songs. For Mabel, these were not merely exercises in memory. She would often stop in mid-hymn and make a brief comment about lyrics she considered particularly relevant to her own situation. I never heard her speak of loneliness or pain except in the stress she placed on certain lines in certain hymns.

It was not many weeks before I turned from a sense that I was being helpful to a sense of wonder, and I would go to her with a pen and paper to write down the things she would say. I have a few of those notes now (I wish I had had the foresight to collect a book full of them), and what follows is the story behind one scrap of paper.

During one hectic week of final exams I was frustrated because my mind seemed to be pulled in ten directions at once with all of the things that I had to think about. The question occurred to me, "What does Mabel have to think about—hour after hour, day after day, week after week, not even able to know if it's day or night?" So I went to her and asked, "Mabel, what do you think about when you lie here?"

And she said, "I think about my Jesus."

I sat there and thought for a moment about the difficulty, for me, of thinking about Jesus for even five minutes, and I asked, "*What* do you think about Jesus?" She replied slowly and deliberately as I wrote. And this is what she said:

> I think about how good he's been to me. He's been awfully good to me in my life, you know. . . . I'm one of those kind who's mostly satisfied. . . . Lots of folks wouldn't care much for what I think. Lots of folks would think I'm kind of old-fashioned. But I don't care. I'd rather have Jesus. He's all the world to me.

And then Mabel began to sing an old hymn:

Jesus is all the world to me,
My life, my joy, my all.
He is my strength from day to day,
Without him I would fall.
When I am sad, to him I go,
No other one can cheer me so.
When I am sad, he makes me glad.
He's my friend.

This is not fiction. Incredible as it may seem, a human being really lived like this. I know. I knew her. *How could she do it?* Seconds ticked and minutes crawled, and so did days and weeks and months and years of pain without human company and without an explanation of why it was all happening—and she lay there and sang hymns. *How could she do it?*

The answer, I think, is that Mabel had something that you and I don't have much of. She had power. Lying there in that bed, unable to move, unable to see, unable to hear, unable to talk to anyone, she had incredible power.

WHAT IS POWER?

When Paul speaks of power, he describes a kind of strength that will enable people to understand what is good and will enable them to do it. In Ephesians 3:14−21 he refers to the energy required to fill people with the knowledge of God so that they can love to such an extent and under such circumstances that are now, at their present level of energy, unthinkable and therefore unaskable. And so he refers in verse 20 to "him who is able to do immeasurably more than all we ask or imagine, according to his power that is at work within us." Similarly, in Colossians 1:10−11, he reveals his prayer for believers: ". . . that you may live a life worthy of the Lord . . . being strengthened with all power according to his glorious might so that you may have great endurance and patience, joyfully giving thanks to the Father." The point is that in Paul's mind, as in his life and as in Mabel's life, the power that he has in view does not generate unusual *production* so much as unusual *persistence*.

Most people fail to understand this, and they operate with a different definition of power. To them, power is the force required to dominate—to dominate people, events, inanimate objects, or money—and often for good ends, for worthy causes. Indeed, we tend to equate the word *power* with those in places of political or intellectual influence.

But for twenty-five years, from Harry Truman to Jimmy Carter, from Josef Stalin to Leonid Brezhnev, while the world's leaders calculated how much force of persuasion or arms or economics would be required to make life what it should be, there in that bed was what life should be. There was power. But nobody asked Mabel.

And for twenty-five years, while scholars and their students argued and wrote and wondered about whether there can be a loving God who would create a world in which there is so much pain, there in that bed was pain. And there was that loving God in all his unthinkable, unaskable power. But nobody asked Mabel.

Well, you might ask, was this really a woman filled with God's power or just a simple-minded country bumpkin with nothing better to do than sing hymns? I'll let you answer that question by suggesting that you conduct a little experiment. The next time you have a headache and a stomach ache, go to bed, close your eyes, and cover your ears with your hands, pressing occasionally to increase the discomfort, and don't move at all. And for an hour, try to do only what Paul describes in Ephesians 3:18–19: "to grasp how wide and long and high and deep is the love of Christ . . . this love that surpasses knowledge." How long do you think you could do it sincerely? Ten minutes? The whole hour? In twenty-five years, there are approximately 170,000 waking hours. How much power would it require to do that for all of that time? And from whom would the power have to come?

Mabel didn't know much, but she did know that what matters most matters every minute. And minutes turn into hours.

THE DEMAND OF POWER

How does one begin to live a life of such power? The first step, I believe, is to recognize the simple but revolutionary truth that such a life is an altogether new life, not merely some kind of "energy supplement." A person may look the same, but everything looks different to that person.

Some sense of this is conveyed by Russian author Alexandr Solzhenitsyn in *The Gulag Archipelago*, his first-hand account of life in the Soviet political prison system. Solzhenitsyn writes about staying alive and sane in the midst of terrible physical and emotional suffering. At one point he describes the most difficult time of all—the interrogation:

> So what is the answer? How can you stand your ground when you are weak and sensitive to pain, when people you love are still alive, when you are unprepared?
>
> What do you need to make you stronger than the interrogator and the whole trap?
>
> From the moment you go to prison you must put your cozy past firmly behind you. At the very threshold, you must say to yourself: "My life is over, a little early to be sure, but there's nothing to be done about it. I shall never return to freedom. I am condemned to die—now or a little later. But later on, in truth, it will be even harder, and so the sooner the better. I no longer have any property whatsoever. For me those I love have died, and for them I have died. From today on, my body is useless and alien to me. Only my spirit and my conscience remain precious and important to me."

> Confronted by such a prisoner, the interrogation will tremble.[1]

Does your interrogator tremble? Perhaps your interrogator is lust, or greed, or anger, or laziness. How long can you hold out against this interrogation, this inexorable power within you working against the good, this enemy who will never let up? Ten minutes? An hour? Twenty-five years? Solzhenitsyn makes the point clearly enough: a life of power demands no less than the sacrifice of that life. The point was made some time earlier by Jesus in words that for many have been rendered meaningless by repetition without demonstration: "Whoever would save his life will lose it; and whoever loses his life for my sake and the gospel's will save it" (Mark 8:35 RSV). It is an all-or-nothing proposition.

THE ACQUISITION OF POWER

The recognition of the extent of the demand involved in a life of power leads to another question. In practical terms, on an ongoing basis, how does one acquire such power? The answer is: Ask for it.

God says that he will give to us the good things that we want if we will only ask (Matt 7:7–11), and power both to choose and to do good is certainly a good thing. The only sure way to know if this promise is true is to try it, to ask honestly and passionately for him to give this good thing. The Book of Psalms provides numerous examples of these prayers of wanting.

But if you are like me, you wonder sometimes what you *do* want, whether you really mean it when you talk about God or when you talk *to* God. Is there any way to assess one's own

---

[1] Alexandr Solzhenitsyn, *The Gulag Archipelago*, 2 vols. (New York, Harper & Row, 1973): 1:130.

desire without playing meaningless mental games of second-guessing?

Consider the example of Isaac Newton. There have been few people in history who have demonstrated such mental power. By 1664 he had mastered all the mathematical works written up to that time. In 1665 he became the first to compute the area of the hyperbola, found the method of approximating series and the rule for reducing any dignity of any binomial into such a series, and discovered calculus. In 1666 he was the first to explain the phenomena of color, and he began the modern science of optics. In the spring of that year he began to develop the theory of gravity and to plot the orbit of the moon, leading eventually to his calculation of the orbits of the entire solar system and some of the comets. Later in 1666—he graduated from college! He was twenty-three years old.

Many years later, an admirer asked Newton how he was able to explain and discover and do so many amazing things. His answer: "By always thinking upon them."

Upon what are you always thinking? Recall the point made in the chapter on prayer: your daydreams are the measure of your values, your goals, your eternity. Your daydreams will tell you what you want, and what you will receive, forever. Are you the hero of that hidden world, ever on stage before ghostly applause? In those daydreams, are you making conquests over enemies, money, lovers? If you are living with that definition of power, you may well get what you want—but that is all, forever.

Or are your daydreams like Mabel's?

Maybe this makes you feel guilty, and you resent that. Who do I think I am, intruding on your conscience this way? The truth is, it is not I. How well I know that I have no right there. I squirm as I write this, revise it, proofread it, and review the final copy before it goes to press. Then perhaps I can put this book aside and take a break from these confrontations with my own inadequacy. But for now I am here with you in the last chapter.

If there is guilt here with us, it is not merely a literary contrivance unless we ignore it, and it is not pathological unless we ignore everything else but it. Guilt can be constructive if it serves as a reminder that we can know what is good and do it. That ability, that power, is offered to us, directly, by Jesus himself. And there are other offers being made by competing forces. Ultimately, we get what we want. But not if our wanting is a spare-time activity for our leisure hours. If it is to be realized, God's power must not be our hobby, but our *obsession*.

> Not that I have already obtained all this, or have already been made perfect, but I press on to take hold of that for which Christ Jesus took hold of me. Brothers, I do not consider myself yet to have taken hold of it. But one thing I do: Forgetting what is behind and straining toward what is ahead, I press on toward the goal to win the prize for which God has called me heavenward in Christ Jesus. (Phil 3:12—14)

• Topical Index •

Readers may wish to follow up on specific themes considered in this book. One way to do this carefully is to use an English concordance that lists the references to each word, usually including a few surrounding words. One drawback of this method is that similar ideas may be represented by different words, and it is easy to miss important references if one does not know all of the synonyms. For example, *possessions, gold,* and *riches* are three of at least a dozen words for wealth. Another drawback is that a high quantity of references, many of which may not be relevant to one's particular interest, presents an intimidating data pool. For example, the word *fear* occurs over one hundred times in the New Testament, but only about one-fourth of those instances refer to fear of God in a positive sense. The purpose of this index, then, is to do some of the "leg work" for the reader who wants to look more closely at certain key topics considered in this book.

References are given in the order of the biblical books, and those that I consider to be key passages are set in boldface type. I have not included every reference under each heading, but I have attempted to supplement the references provided in the book with enough material to give a fairly comprehensive picture of each topic.

INTRODUCTION
The command to love God and its relation to conduct **Deut 6:4–7**; 11:1–32; John 14:15–24; **1 John 2:3–6**; 3:15; 4:3.

The command to love one's neighbor and one's fellow believer **Lev 19:18**; Matt 7:21–27; 25:31–46; **Mark 12:28–34**; Luke 11:15–37; John 13:34–35; 15:12–17; Rom 12:10; 13:8–10; Gal 5:13–14; 6:10; Eph 4:15–16; Col 3:14; Heb 10:24; James 2:14–17; 1 Peter 1:22; 2:17; 1 John 3:17–18; 4:7–12, 20–21.

The ethic of striving Matt 5:17–20; 5:48; Luke 13:24; 1 Cor 9:24–25; 14:12; **Phil 3:12–14**; Col 1:29; 1 Tim 4:7b–10; 6:11–12; Heb 5:11–6:1; 12:12–14; 2 Peter 1:5–11.

CHAPTER ONE

Humility before God Job 42:1–6; Ps 51:1–19; 139:1-18: Isa 57:15; 66:2; Jer 23:23–24; Mic 6:8; **Matt 5:3**; 23:12; Luke 18:9–14; Rom 7:21–25; 1 Peter 5:6.

Fear of God Deut 5:29; 6:2, 13, 24; Job 1:1; Ps 2:11; 19:9; 130:4; Prov 1:7; 3:7; 9:10; Isa 11:2–3; Luke 1:50; 7:16; 12:5; Acts 2:43; 9:31; Rom 11:20; 2 Cor 5:11; Phil 2:12; Col 3:22; Heb 5:7; 1 Peter 1:17; 2:17; Rev 14:7; 19:5; compare with Matt 14:26–27; Rom 8:15; Heb 2:15; 1 John 4:18.

CHAPTER TWO

Joy Ezra 3:11–13; Ps 16:7–9; 32:11; 65:13; 71:23; Isa 12:6; 42:11; 66:10–11; Zec 9:9; Luke 1:14; 6:23; 10:20; Rom 12:12; 15:13; Gal 5:22; Eph 5:18–20; Phil 2:17–18; 4:4; Col 1:11–14; 1 Thess 5:16; 1 Peter 1:6–9; 4:13; Jude 24–25; Rev 19:6–8.

Peace Lev 26:1–6; Ps 4:7–8; 119:165–66; Isa 26:3; 32:15–19; Ezek 34:25–31; Zec 8:11–13; Luke 1:76–79; John 14:27; 16:33; Rom 5:1; 8:6; 14:17; 15:13; Gal 5:22; Eph 2:14–18; Phil 4:7; 1 Thess 5:23; 2 Thess 3:16; Heb 13:20; 1 Peter 1:2.

CHAPTER THREE

Prayer and subjects of prayer 2 Chron 7:14–15; Ps 25:1–7; 51:11–19; 69:1–36; 86:1–17; 102:1–11; 103:1–22; **Matt 6:9–13**; Mark 11:25; 14:32–42; Luke 10:2; 11:5–13; 18:1–8; 22:32; John 17:1–26; Acts 7:60; 28:8; Rom 8:26; 12:12; 15:30–32; 1 Cor 14:1–25; 2 Cor 1:11; 12:8; 13:7–9; Eph 1:16–18; 3:14–19; 6:18–20; Phil 1:3–5, 9–11; 4:6; Col 1:3–4, 9–12; 4:2–4, 12; 1 Thess 1:2–3; 5:17; 2 Thess 1:11–12; 3:1–2; 1 Tim 2:1–4; Phm 1:4–6; Heb 5:7; James 5:13–18; 1 John 1:9.

The promise of answered prayer Ps 30:1–12; 32:1–5; 40:1–10; 65:1–4; 118:1–9; Prov 15:8; **Matt 7:7–11**; 18:19; 21:22; Mark 11:24; John 14:13–14; 15:7, 16; 16:23–24; 1 John 3:22; 5:14–16.

CHAPTER FOUR

Wealth and its renunciation as dependence on God Deut 8:17–18; Job 22:23–30; Ps 49:16–17; 73:1–12; Prov 8:10; 11:4; 22:6; 23:4; Eccl 5:10–12; Jer 5:26–28; 12:1; Matt 5:40–42; **6:19–34**; 13:44–46; Mark 1:16–20; 2:14; 4:19; 6:8–9; 8:34–37; **10:17–31**; 12:41–44; 14:8–9; Luke 6:20–25; 12:13–21; 14:18–20, 25–33; 16:1–12, 14–15, 19–31; 17:28–33; 19:1–10; Acts 2:44–45; 4:32–5:11; 1 Cor 7:30; 13:3; Phil 4:11–12; 1 Tim 6:6–10, 17–19; Heb 13:5–7; James 2:2–7; 5:1–5; Rev 3:15–18.

CHAPTER FIVE

Sympathy Exod 22:27; Ps 51:1; 145:9; Isa 49:13; 54:1–10; Hos 11:1–9; Matt 9:36; 14:14; 15:32; Mark 1:41; Luke 7:13; 19:41; John 11:1–36; Rom 12:15; 2 Cor 1:3; **2 Cor 1:3–11**; **7:5–16**; Gal 6:2; Eph 4:32; Phil 2:1; Col 3:12–13; Heb 4:15; 1 Peter 3:8.

CHAPTER SIX

Unity among believers Mark 10:29–30; John 17:11; Acts 2:44–46; 4:32–35; Rom 12:3–8; 15:5–6; 1 Cor 12:12–26; **Eph 4:1–16**; **Phil 2:1–2**; Col 3:12–17.

CHAPTER SEVEN

Service and submission Matt 20:25–28; Mark 10:45; 14:3–9; Luke 8:1–3; **John 13:8–15**; Rom 12:7; 14:13–23; 1 Cor 12:4–11; 16:15–16; 2 Cor 8:9; Gal 5:22; 6:1–10; Eph 4:32; 5:21–6:9; **Phil 2:1–11**; Col 3:12, 18–25; 1 Tim 2:8–3:13; 5:1–6:2; Titus 2:1–10; Heb 6:10; 13:17; 1 Peter 2:18; 3:1–7; 5:5.

CHAPTER EIGHT

Verbal nurture Matt 18:15–17; Rom 12:8; 1 Cor 14:1–4; 2 Cor 10:8; Eph 4:1, 9–16, 29; 5:4, 19–20; Col 3:16–17; 4:6; 1 Thess 3:2–3; 4:18; 5:11; 2 Thess 3:14–15; 1 Tim 5:20; 2 Tim 4:1–2; Titus 3:2, 10–11; Heb 3:13, 12:5; 13:22; 1 Peter 5:1–3.

CHAPTER NINE

The centrality of suffering Isa 53:1–10; Matt 5:10–12; Mark 8:34–38; John 15:18–21; Rom 5:3–5; 8:17; Phil 1:29; 3:10; Heb 2:10–18; **12:1–11**; 1 Peter 1:5–9; **2:18–25**; 4:12–13.

Kinds of suffering Matt 5:4, 10–12; Mark 10:28–30; 13:9–13; Luke 9:57–62; 14:26–33; Rom 12:14–21; 2 Cor 1:3–11; Gal 5:22–23; Eph 5:21–6:9; Col 3:18–4:1; 2 Tim 3:12; 1 Peter 2:18–24; 3:13–17; 4:1–5, 14–16; Rev 2:9–10.

CHAPTER TEN

Patience and forgiveness Exod 23:4–5; Prov 17:13; 20:22; 24:17–18, 29; 25:21; Matt 5:21–26; **5:38–47**; 6:14–15; 7:1–5; 18:21–35; 26:51–52; Mark 14:60–15:5; Luke 6:27–36; 10:25–37; 14:12–14; 17:3–4; 23:34; **Rom 12:14–21**; 1 Cor 4:12; 13:4; 2 Cor 2:5–11; 10:1; Gal 5:22; 6:1–5; Eph 4:1–3, 26–27; 31–32; Col 3:8, 12–13; 1 Thess 5:15; James 1:19–21; 3:10, 17; 4:11–12; 1 Peter 2:18–25; 3:9–17; 4:14–16; 1 John 2:9–11; 3:15–18; 4:20–21.

CHAPTER ELEVEN

Boldness in communicating one's faith Matt 4:19; **5:16**; 5:19; 10:19–20, 27; 28:19; Mark 6:7–13; Luke 10:2; John 4:7–42; 9:1–40; 15:26–27; 17:20; Acts 1:8; 2:14–40; 4:29–31; 5:17–32; 8:1, 4; 17:22–31; 19:30; 26:24–29; Rom 12:6–8; 1 Cor 12:28; 2 Cor 3:12; Eph 4:11; Phil 1:12–14, 27–29; Col 4:5–6; 1 Thess 1:8; 4:11–12; 2 Tim 4:5; Titus 2:7–8; 3:2; 1 Peter 2:9, 12; 3:15; 4:14.

CHAPTER TWELVE

Self-control over sensual appetites Mark 7:21; Luke 21:34; Rom 13:13; 1 Cor 6:12–13; 9:24–27; 2 Cor 12:21; Gal 5:19–23; Eph 4:19; 1 Thess 4:3–8; Titus 1:8; 1 Peter 4:3; 2 Peter 1:6; 2:2. The boundaries of biblical sexuality Lev 18:22; 20:13; Matt 5:27–32; 19:3–12; Rom 1:27–28; 1 Cor 6:9–20; 7:1–40; 1 Tim 1:10; 2 Peter 2:6–7; Jude 7; compare with Gen 1:27–31; 2:20–24; Eph 5:25–33.